MAKING SENSE IN THE SOCIAL SCIENCES

a student's guide
to research, writing, and style

Margot Northey & Lorne Tepperman

Toronto
Oxford University Press

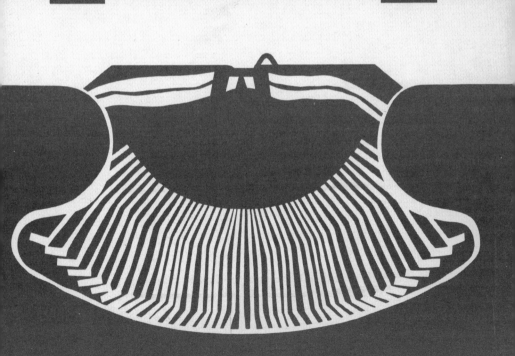

Oxford University Press, 70 Wynford Drive, Don Mills, Ontario, M3C 1J9

Toronto Oxford New York Delhi Bombay Calcutta Madras Karachi
Petaling Jaya Singapore Hong Kong Tokyo Nairobi Dar es Salaam
Cape Town Melbourne Auckland

and associated companies in
Berlin Ibadan

Canadian Cataloguing in Publication Data
Northey, Margot Elizabeth
Making sense in the social sciences: a student's
guide to writing and style

Includes index.
ISBN 0-19-540544-7

1. Exposition (Rhetoric).   2. Social sciences—
Authorship.   3. Report writing.   4. English language—
Rhetoric).   I. Tepperman, Lorne.
II. Title.

H91.N67 1986   808'.0663021   C86-093841-7

Contents

Acknowledgements

The portion of this book concerned with research design and interpretation benefitted considerably from the efforts of many readers. Professor Jim Curtis (Waterloo) and Jack Richardson (McMaster) read and commented extensively on two drafts of this material. Other friends—Jean Guillaume, John Hagan, Charles Jones, Dennis Magill, Bill Michelson, Eric Single and Sandra Wain—offered useful suggestions at various stages of the project. As well, fourteen undergraduate students in my Introduction to Sociology course reviewed the first draft for clarity and simplicity of expression. I want to thank all of these readers and helpers for making the book better than it would have been otherwise. Of course, I remain responsible for the flaws: for roads not taken and other misjudgements.

Brian Timney's section on word-processing from *Making Sense in Psychology and the Life Sciences* has been included in this book, and I wish to thank him for the use of it. I also wish to acknowledge the use of the following diagrams: 'Path Diagram' simplified from Michael Ornstein 'The Occupational Mobility of Men in Ontario' in *Canadian Review of Sociology and Anthropology* 18(2) 1981, used by permission of the author and the publisher. 'A model of relationships between demographic, social and economic change in a pre-industrial society' from E.A. Wrigley *Population and History*, World University Library (1969), used by permission of McGraw-Hill Book Company, New York. 'The Research Cycle' from Peter Li 'Methods of Sociology Research' in *The Social World: An Introduction to Sociology* by Lorne Tepperman and Jack Richardson, used by permission of McGraw-Hill Ryerson Limited. 'Simplified Gouldner Model' from James March and Herbert Simon, *Organizations*, used by permission of John Wiley and Sons. 'Qualitative and Quantitative Paradigms' from Charles S. Reichardt and Thomas D. Cook 'Beyond Qualitative versus Quantitative Methods' in T.D. Cook and C.S. Reichardt, eds., *Qualitative and Quantitative Methods in Evaluation Research*, Beverly Hills, Sage Publications, 1979.

On the production side, I am grateful to Richard Teleky and Sally Livingston at Oxford. Richard gave me a free hand, but supplied encouragement and suggestions whenever needed. Sally prodded me gently but firmly on details of exposition. It was a real pleasure working with both of them.

The book is dedicated to all well-intentioned undergraduates. They struggle daily to understand how social science is different from common sense and arm-chair speculation, on the one hand, and jargon-filled data juggling, on the other. I hope this book will make sense of it for them.

Symbols for common errors

NOTE: If any of the following markings appear on one of your essays
or reports, consult Chapter 8 or 9, or the Glossary, for help.

agr	agreement of subject and verb
amb	ambiguity
awk	awkwardness
cap	capitalization
cs	comma splice
D	diction
dang	dangling modifier (*or* dm)
frag	sentence fragment
gr	grammar or usage
mod	misplaced modifier
¶	new paragraph
//	parallelism
P	punctuation
quot	quotation marks
ref	pronoun reference
rep	repetition
RO	run-on sentence
sp	spelling
SS	sentence structure
sp inf	split infinitive
sub	subordination
T	tense
trans	transition
⌒	transpose (change order of letters or words)
wdy	wordy
ww	wrong word

A note to the student

Contrary to many students' belief, good writing does not come naturally; even for the best writers it's mostly hard work, following the old formula of ten per cent inspiration and ninety per cent perspiration.

Writing in university or college is not fundamentally different from writing elsewhere. Yet each piece of writing has its own special purposes, and these are what determine its particular substance, shape, and tone. *Making Sense in the Social Sciences* will examine both the general precepts for effective writing and the special requirements of social-science research; it will also point out some of the most common errors in student composition and suggest how to avoid or correct them. Written mostly in the form of guidelines rather than strict rules—since few rules are inviolable— this book should help you escape the common pitfalls of student writing and develop confidence through an understanding of basic principles and a mastery of sound techniques.

Preface

This book is intended to teach students how to write good term papers, examinations, and research reports for social-science courses. Writing well in the social sciences demands not only a good writing style, but also a good understanding of research design, theory, measurement, argument, and communication. All these qualities must be present in order for you to get your ideas across clearly and persuasively.

Books on student writing rarely deal with the issues discussed in the first half of this guide. Since many authors believe they belong more properly to the topic of research methods, too often these ideas are segregated into specialized, hard-to-read books. Many students treat them as though they were hard to understand and practice routinely; but they are not. Moreover, they are basic to good social-science writing—fundamental to "making sense" to your teacher and other readers. For this reason these ideas need to be learned and cultivated in every social-science course.

Much of what appears in the following chapters is written as though you were conducting and describing a research project of your own. But the same principles apply, with equal force, to understanding (making sense of), describing, and criticizing the work of any other social scientist, amateur or professional. (A more explicit guide to reviewing other people's work is provided in Chapter 9, on writing book reports.)

Thus the discussion that follows has two related goals. One is to show you how to do research yourself: research that makes sense to a reader who may not already be persuaded of your views. The other is to show you how to make sense of other researchers' work, in order to use and evaluate their findings in essays, book reviews, and examination answers. Clearly, these two goals are two sides of the same coin.

Making sense in the social sciences is similar, in many ways, to making sense in the physical sciences and humanities. But some of the problems described here are more marked in the social sciences, which use more varied research methods than the physical sciences and humanities. Some problems are unique to particular social sciences, but many others are not. Only the common ones are discussed here, using examples from all the social sciences. Exercises are included at regular intervals, and at the end of the book, to illustrate this variety of research problems.

Chapters 2 to 6 of this book approach research as though it were mainly of the survey variety: that is, focusing on the examination of relationships between measured variables, using questionnaire or interview data. This approach is justifiable on two grounds. First, a great deal of social-science research is in fact of the survey variety (as opposed to the historical, field-observation, experimental, or literature-synthesizing varieties). Second, and more important, basic ideas about research design, data analysis, and so on can be grasped most easily in relation to surveys, and then applied with slight modification to other kinds of research. Some discussions of participant or field observation are included in the text below, and strategies of library research receive explicit attention in Chapter 7.

Throughout the first half of the book you will find exercises designed to get you to apply the new ideas we are presenting. Don't worry if they touch on topics you are not familiar with — remember, this book is aimed at all of the social sciences. Make a stab at each problem, considering alternative approaches and sources of data. They are all "good problems" in the sense that they permit a variety of solutions; and many have been vigorously debated for years. This is your chance to join in the debates.

The value of what is presented here is not limited to writing good term papers, exams, and research projects. More sensible communication in the social sciences is useful outside school as well: in government, in business, even in analysing the events of everyday life. We hope you will use the principles learned from this book long after you have stopped writing papers that only a professor will read.

1
Writing
and thinking

You are not likely to produce clear writing unless you have first done some clear thinking, and thinking can't be hurried. It follows that the most important step you can take is to leave yourself enough time to think.

Psychologists have shown that we don't always solve a difficult problem by "putting our mind to it"—by determined reasoning. Sometimes when we are stuck it's best to take a break, sleep on it, and let the subconscious or creative part of our brain take over for a while. Very often a period of relaxation will produce a new approach or solution. Just remember that leaving time for creative reflection isn't the same thing as sitting around listening to the stereo until inspiration strikes out of the blue.

INITIAL STRATEGIES

To write is to make choices. Practice makes the decisions easier to come by, but no matter how fluent you become, with each piece of writing you will still have to choose.

You can narrow the field of choice from the start if you realize that you are *not* writing for anybody, anywhere, for no particular reason. In university (or anywhere else), it's always sound strategy to ask yourself two basic questions: "What is the purpose of this piece of writing?" and "What is the reader like?" Your first reaction may be "Well, I'm writing for my teacher to satisfy a course requirement." But that's not specific enough. To be useful, your answers have to be precise.

Think about the purpose

Your purpose may be any one or two of several possibilities:
- to show that you understand certain terms or theories;
- to show that you can do independent research;
- to apply a specific theory to new material;
- to provide information;
- to show your knowledge of a topic or text;
- to show that you can think critically or creatively.

Certainly an assignment designed to see if you have read and understood specific material calls for a different approach from one that's meant to test your critical thinking or research skills. If you don't determine the exact purpose, you may find yourself working at cross purposes—and wasting a lot of time.

Think about the reader

Thinking about the reader does *not* mean playing up to the teacher. To convince a particular person that your own views are sound, you have to consider his or her way of thinking. If you are writing a paper on Israeli communes for a sociology professor, obviously your analysis will be different from what it would be if you were writing for an economics or history professor. You will have to make specific decisions about the terms you should explain, the background information you should supply, and the details you need to convince that particular reader. In the same way, if your reader supports the idea of a common market between Canada and the United States and you intend to propose higher tariffs, you will have to anticipate any arguments that may be raised, in order to answer them. If you don't know who will be reading your paper—your professor, your tutorial leader, or a marker—just imagine someone intelligent, knowledgeable, and interested, skeptical enough to question your ideas but flexible enough to adopt them if your evidence is convincing.

Think about the length

Before you start writing, you will also need to think about the length of your assignment in relation to the time you have available to spend on it. If both the topic and the length are prescribed, it should be fairly easy for you to assess the level of detail required and the amount of research you need to do. If only the length is prescribed, that restriction will help you decide how broad or how narrow a topic you should choose (see p. 113).

Think about the tone

In everyday writing to friends you probably take a casual tone, but academic writing is usually more formal. The exact degree of formality required will depend on the kind of assignment and instruction you have been given. In some cases — say, if your psychology professor asks you to express yourself freely and personally in a journal — you may well be able to use an informal style. Essays and reports, however, require a more formal tone. What kind of style is too informal for most academic work? Here are the main signs:

Use of slang

Although the occasional slang word or phrase may be useful for special effect, frequent use of slang is not acceptable. The reason is that slang expressions are usually regional and short-lived: they may mean different things to different groups at different times. (Just think of how widely the meanings of *hot* and *cool* can vary, depending on the circumstances.)

Excessive use of first-person pronouns

Since a formal essay is not a personal outpouring, you want to keep it from becoming *I*-centred. It's certainly acceptable to use the occasional first-person pronoun, and your reader will obviously want to know your opinions—as long as they are backed by evidence. Still, you should avoid the *I think* or *in my view* approach when the fact or argument speaks for itself. If the choice, however, is between using *I* and creating a tangle of passive constructions, it's almost always better to choose *I*. (A hint: when you do use *I*, it will be less noticeable if you place it in the middle of the sentence rather than at the beginning.)

Frequent use of contractions

Generally speaking, contractions such as *can't* and *isn't* are not suitable for academic writing, although they may be fine for letters or other informal kinds of writing—for example, this handbook. The problem with trying to avoid excessive informality is that you may be tempted to go to the other extreme. If your writing sounds stiff or pompous, you may be using too many high-flown phrases, long words, or passive constructions (see Chapter 11).

2
Design

Once you have thought about the purpose of your work, and your reader, the next step is to think about design. As noted in the Preface, the principles of good research design are valuable not only in conducting and reporting good research, but also in interpreting and criticizing the work of others. The suggestions that follow are sometimes written as though you, the student, were designing your own project, but they can also be used to understand, describe, and criticize research that someone else has done. In this way they can help to improve your ability to "make sense" in a book report, examination answer, or literature review. And although our discussion is based on survey research, which provides the simplest model of what research design and analysis are aiming at, the points made are just as relevant to library research or field observation (see Chapter 4 for a discussion of these different ways of collecting data).

Good design is fundamental to good research. By "good design" we mean planning a project in advance to produce results that are persuasive. Good design is just as important to a social scientist as to an architect or engineer; without it, what you construct can't stand up for long. A badly designed research project cannot produce a well-argued, sensible report or examination answer because its results will not really answer the question you are trying to address. Knowing the question you are trying to answer, and the types of data and analysis that would best answer it, is the essence of good design.

It's not always easy to identify the basic requirements of a research project. Much social-science research suggests that bad design is the single most common cause of bad, "nonsensical" research findings. That is why we are discussing design first, and at some length.

This chapter will examine the four main types of research design and point out the dangers of mixing them, or of ignoring design concerns outright. The material may initially seem difficult, but only because it is unfamiliar and uses an unfamiliar vocabulary (a glossary of important terms is provided at the end of the book). After reading and thinking about it, you will find the points made here clear and perhaps even obvious.

STARTING POINTS

Choose a good problem

The first step towards doing any good work is choosing a problem that is worth working on: a topic of some theoretical or practical importance; a topic of interest to you, the writer, who must invest considerable time and effort to complete the task; and yet a problem that is small enough to be studied in a craftsmanlike way in the time available. Overreaching yourself—starting more than you can finish well; overestimating your real interest in the problem; or spending a lot of effort answering a question that is, when looked at objectively, not really worth answering—will not produce worthwhile results.

Know the type of design you are using

Different designs have typical patterns, and if you deviate from the appropriate pattern for the design you have chosen, chances are great you will not answer the question that is, or should be, of central interest. For example, if your goal is to understand the *causes* of problem drinking (or the Second World War, or the location of cities), describing the *effects* of problem drinking (or the Second World War, or the location of cities) should take a distinctly secondary place. (Of course, it is sometimes difficult to distinguish between causes and consequences; more will be said about this in the discussion of systemic design.)

Equally, if you have focused your energy on *describing* the lives of problem drinkers, the events of the Second World War, or the characteristics of cities located along rivers, you may not have collected information that is relevant to *explaining* the *causes* of those phenomena. In that case, don't attempt to explain them. Be aware of "goal displacement," and don't overreach your data or expect them to tell you things they cannot; otherwise all you will produce is unfounded speculation. Worse, you will rob your real task—description, in this case—of the time and effort needed to do a good job.

TYPES OF DESIGNS

There are many ways to describe and categorize research designs. Courses on theory and research method will introduce you to other useful categorizations, but in the meantime the method discussed below will help you make sense of your own and other people's research goals.

For our present purposes, the four main types of research design are relational, predictive, explanatory, and systemic. These four types are defined in terms of how many dependent and independent variables each is examining. Before proceeding, therefore, we must define these different types of variables.

Types of variables

A *variable* is a characteristic or condition that can differ from one person, group, or situation to another. (The persons being described are called the *units of analysis*.) So, for example, we might select twenty political-science majors (our units of analysis) at a given university and from each collect such information as grade average, age, gender, and participation in campus politics. These characteristics are variables in the sense that they can vary among the people we are studying.

A *dependent variable* is a characteristic or condition that is changed by changes in another variable: it is assumed to be the *effect* of an independent or causal variable. In this case, level of participation in campus politics is the dependent variable we are hoping to explain through reference to three independent variables: age, gender, and grades. An *independent variable* is a causal or explanatory variable: a condition or characteristic that is presumed to be the *cause* of changes in the dependent variable.

In the present instance, we could examine whether variations in age, gender, or grade average appeared to influence campus political participation: that is, whether males participated more than females, older students more than younger ones, and students with higher grade averages more than students with lower grade averages.

A third type of variable is the intervening variable. An *intervening variable* is, as its name suggests, one that intervenes between the independent and dependent variable. It is the *means by which* the independent variable exerts its influence on the dependent variable. For a variable to be considered "intervening" it must be influenced by the independent variable and influence the dependent variable. Thus it must be both an effect of the initial cause and a cause of the subsequent effect.

For example, consider the question of how people achieve the job status they do in modern societies: that is, their "status attainment." It has been observed that the status attained by adults (specifically, sons) is very similar to the status attained by their parents (specific-ally, fathers). What is the mechanism by which this occurs? Some argue that it is higher education: that is, education is the intervening variable. A father's status will determine how much education the son receives; and how much education the son receives will, in turn, determine the status he attains as an adult. To demonstrate that this process is what actually occurs, and that education *is* the intervening variable through which father's status influences son's status, a sim-ple test is needed. That is to "control for" education. If education really is the intervening variable we believe it to be, we must be able to show that people with the same amount of education will achieve the same adult job status, regardless of their father's status. In other words, education will make the original relationship between father's and son's status disappear; boys from very different class backgrounds who receive the same amount of education will achieve the same level of adult status. (Note that we are not discussing girls and women here; female status attainment is quite different from male status attain-ment, for reasons too numerous to go into here.)

A fourth type of variable is what we shall call the *conditioning variable*. This is a variable that determines the conditions under which the independent variable will have a strong or weak, positive or nega-tive effect on the dependent variable. Unlike the intervening variable, the conditioning variable is not an effect of the independent variable but is quite independent of it. Nor is it a cause of the dependent variable. The conditioning variable, which may suppress, magnify, or otherwise distort the relationship between independent and dependent variable, sets the conditions under which cause will determine effects.

Consider the horrible problem of death through starvation in Africa. Death is not a direct result of inadequate transportation, but rather of a continued, massive crop failure. The dependent variable is death through starvation; the independent variable, the availability of food. Outsiders might try to influence the dependent variable by manipu-lating the independent variable: that is, by increasing the food sup-ply through international shipments of food. Such a strategy worked well in Europe after the Second World War; but it is not working well in Africa today, because the conditions under which it could work are not being met.

Among many others, these conditions include an adequate trans-portation system. Because of poor roads and railways, food supplies sent from abroad are piling up in warehouses far from the people who need them. One concludes that the problem of death through starvation is the result not merely of a crop's failing or the unavailability of aid, but rather of the interaction of crop shortage and bad transportation. Neither good transportation nor available food taken alone will solve the problem: they must both be present. Stated otherwise, good transportation is the condition under which imported food will influence the death rate. Transportation adequacy is, then, the conditioning variable.

In short, independent variables are what we are considering *causes*; dependent variables, what we are considering *effects*. The numbers of presumed causes and effects define the type of research design to be followed. Since any piece of research can examine one or many causes and one or many effects, four types of design are logically possible. They are depicted in Figure 2.1.

Figure 2.1

TYPES OF RESEARCH DESIGN

NUMBER OF "CAUSES" OR INDEPENDENT VARIABLES

		One	Two or More
	ONE	Relational Study	Explanatory Study
Number of "effects" or Dependent Variables	TWO OR MORE	Predictive Study	Systemic Study

We shall consider these types of design in order, going from the simplest (the relational) to the most complex (the systemic). First, though, try your hand at the following exercise.

EXERCISE 1

Causes and effects

Is religion a strong moral and social force in Canada today?

1. Reword the question in a way that identifies the "causes" and the "effects."
2. What are some reasons why, in answering this question, you should not try to explain the causes of religiosity?
3. What independent variable and what dependent variables do you need to study in order to answer this question?

Relational studies

Relational studies examine one cause and one effect, and the conditions under which the relationship between them is strong or weak, positive or negative. In a *strong* relationship, a large change in one variable produces a large change in the other; in a *weak* relationship, a large change in one variable produces only a small change in the other. In a *positive* relationship, two variables increase and decrease together; in a *negative* relationship, as one variable increases, the other decreases.

It is the purpose of a relational study to examine variables that suppress or magnify the effect of the independent variable. For example, take the case of suicide rates, a classic sociological concern. Researchers have long known that suicide rates differ between men and women, and by marital status. One gender seems more suicide-prone than the other; and one marital status, more suicide-producing than another. Taken individually these independent variables do not produce very strong effects. Taken together, however, they do. Some researchers have shown that the suicide rate is highest for married females and single males, and much lower for single females and married males. Thus the relationship between suicide rate and gender is mediated by, or interacts with, marital status. Marital status is the conditioning variable here; marriage tends to suppress the probability of suicide in males and increase it in females. To discover why, we must investigate the nature of modern marriage.

This kind of investigation, identifying and exploring the context within which an independent variable has the effect it does, is a standard example of a relational study. But within this group there are various subtypes. One of the most important is the following.

Deviant-case analysis

The deviant-case analysis examines people or groups who appear to violate some accepted theory. In the deviant case, a cause that usually produces a particular effect produces a different effect (or no effect at all). The researcher's purpose, as in the suicide study above, is to discover what variable is changing the usual effect of the independent variable.

An example is the study by S.M. Lipset et al., *Union Democracy* (1956). Lipset was interested in the conditions that made democratic government possible in the light of the "iron law of oligarchy" stated by sociologist Robert Michels many decades earlier: that every organization (and state), no matter how democratic at the outset, would tend in the long run to "oligarchy," the seizure of control and undemocratic decision-making by a small leadership group.

Lipset believed that this tendency to oligarchy could be suppressed, making democracy possible, under certain conditions. The problem was to discover those conditions. To do so, Lipset studied a deviant case: the International Typographer's Union, a union of printers reputed to be highly democratic in its decision-making practices. After investigating the history and organization of the union, and the attitudes and practices of both its leaders and its rank and file, he reached certain conclusions about the conditions for political democracy, which he later generalized in his book *Political Man* (1963).

Predictive studies

In our terminology, predictive studies are those that examine one cause and two or more effects. A great deal of pure research and most applied research is predictive in this sense. The many subtypes differ in one main way: that is, in whether the causal variable under consideration is identified by a theory, as in pure research; or by a policy (e.g., organization mandate, resources, or feasibility), as in applied research.

Predictive studies with causes defined by theory

The theoretical, or pure-research, group includes speculative studies, experiments, and quasi-experiments.

Speculative studies. These imagine the effects of an independent variable on many dependent variables. Since they are imaginative, they are sometimes called *thought experiments*, and are carried out by applying some loose theory, or intuition, to a combination of imagined and real data. We could put Plato's *Republic* or More's *Utopia* in this category; a more recent example is Michael Young's *Rise of the Meritocracy*. Such studies might attempt to answer questions like the following: How would Canadian society differ if no one ever died? What would have happened in the Second World War if the atom bomb had not been invented? How would the geographic distribution of people in Canada change if people could transport themselves instantly from one place to another? How would people use their time if no one had to work?

Such speculations share certain common features: they all examine one independent variable and attempt to predict, or speculate about, its many likely effects; all can be informed, but not tested, by observable data; and all require that the researcher understand, theoretically, the connections between independent and dependent variables in the real world.

Good speculation must take into account what is already known. For example, the likely effects of people living forever can be at least partly predicted by the already observable effects of a longer life expectancy. The effects of people not having to work at all can be at least partly predicted by the observable effects of increased leisure on modern life-style. What is not known is whether the condition speculated about will simply continue what is already happening, or whether, after a certain critical point, relationships between the independent and dependent variables will change in dramatic, unforeseeable ways.

Experiments. These study the observable effects of actual interventions. They test the predictions made by a closely reasoned theory, often using a small-scale "model" of the situation being studied. In many cases, the direction and approximate size of expected outcomes is specified in advance. Doing this type of research usually requires laboratory work (to minimize outside influence), controlled data collection (including random or unbiased sampling of the people to be studied, and precise measurement), and quantitative data and analysis. Real experiments differ from thought experiments both in the precision with which they are executed and in the possibility of verifying predictions.

The classical experiment is considered by many the ideal means of testing a relationship between dependent and independent variables. Even though experimentation is not possible in most of the social sciences, familiarity with the experimental approach will give the reader a better sense of what researchers are hoping to achieve by other means.

In a typical experiment there are two groups or *conditions*: the *experimental condition*, in which subjects will be manipulated in some way that is predicted to have a certain effect on their behaviour; and the *control condition*, in which subjects will *not* be manipulated in this way. In order to see how much the experimental manipulation changes people's behaviour we need a baseline, or measure of the behaviour before the experimental manipulation takes place. This is the purpose of the control group — one that is identical in all important respects except that it does not receive the experimental manipulation. If the experimental group changes more than the control group, that change can then be attributed to the experimental manipulation.

Consider the following example. An experimenter wants to test the theory that drunken behaviour is not the result of alcohol acting on the body chemistry, but a result of people's expectations about alcohol's effects and a desire to take advantage of the deviance that drunkenness legitimates.

The hypothesis is that people who think they have consumed an alcohol-like substance will act more drunkenly than people who think they have consumed a coffee-like substance (who are hypothesized to behave in a more than usually "sober" manner). People who know nothing about the expected effects of the substance they have consumed (i.e., the control group) are hypothesized to behave less drunkenly than the first group and less soberly than the second.

Three groups of undergraduates, randomly sampled from a psychology class, agree to participate. Individual subjects are tested on a simulated automobile driving task for five minutes each, to establish their base-line driving skill. Then each is administered a "placebo," that is, a chemically inert substance — in this case, a capsule filled with sugar.

Each is given "information" about the expected effects of the capsule they have ingested; and after a twenty-minute interval each is directed to drive the simulated automobile for another five minutes.

The change in driving skills is measured for each subject, and an average change score calculated for each of the three groups. The finding? The "alcohol group" felt drunk, the "coffee group" sober; but there was no significant difference observed in their driving skills: the alcohol group did not drive worse, nor the coffee group better than the control group after taking their capsules. The experimenter therefore rejects the hypothesis as invalid.

Quasi-experiments. Like experiments, these study the observable effects of actual interventions, but they exercise less control over the research setting—more often a field setting than a laboratory—and the selection of subjects. Put another way, quasi-experiments are carried out where true experiments cannot be, because subjects cannot be completely controlled. This is not to say that quasi-experiments are sloppy, or "merely" speculative. They often involve very precise data collection. And they can prove very useful in analysing how behaviours change over time. Yet they are not quite experiments.

To take the influence of outside factors into account, quasi-experiments also use control or comparison groups. For example, consider a quasi-experiment to assess the effect of increased policing on the occurrence of robberies in a community. Researchers collect data on the robbery rate for six months before and six months after an increase in the numbers of policemen or hours of police surveillance. As well, they observe a comparison community that is similar in all important respects (e.g., population and class composition) except that it has not increased its policing. The researchers collect robbery data from both communities for the same twelve-month period, and then compare changes in robbery rate in the two communities. If the rate declines more in the first (experimental) than in the second (comparison) community, we have grounds for thinking that the decline was *caused* by increased policing, the only apparent relevant difference between the communities. (Similar studies have been done to measure the effectiveness of seat-belt and speeding legislation.)

The problem is that the researchers cannot have selected the experimental or comparison communities randomly, or prevented other changes in these communities that might also contribute to the observed difference: for example, changes in prosperity, employment rate, or the reporting of robberies by victims. For these reasons the quasi-experiment yields a weaker conclusion than the experiment, but a conclusion that is nonetheless more secure than that provided by research without the before-and-after measurement, the comparison or control group, and the rigorous collection and analysis of observable data.

EXERCISE 2

Prediction

What implication does the increase in single-parent families have for society?

1. Reword this question in order to identify the "causes" and the "effects."

2. What kind of predictive study is called for: speculative, experimental, or quasi-experimental? Why?
3. What information would you collect to answer this question?

Predictive studies with causes defined by policy

The policy, or applied-research, group includes social-impact assessments, demonstration projects, and evaluation studies.

Social-impact assessments. These predict the likely effects of a policy intervention, using a combination of thought experiment, expert opinion, and surveyed public opinion. They attempt to determine how people would react to these effects and, given their likely extent and seriousness, what course of action should be pursued: this one, or another (similarly analysed), or none at all.

In recent years, social-impact assessments have been conducted in many oil-producing regions of the world (including Alberta, Newfoundland, and Scotland) to predict the probable impact of oil extraction on the surrounding area. Such assessments have paid attention to likely effects on the environment, local economy, community organization, and way of life. Such predictions are influential in deciding where, how, and how quickly to develop the oil-resource industry.

Demonstration projects. These resemble quasi-experiments, but they are motivated by policy, not theoretical, concerns. They study the effects of actual interventions in a natural field setting. Here too the choice of intervention is determined by political and organizational feasibility. Deciding whether to continue and increase the scope of intervention is based on observed, not anticipated, impacts.

For example, suppose that a government ministry decides to keep fewer inmates in prisons. It is believed that some kind of halfway house may help released prisoners adjust to normal life better than if they are simply and suddenly released into the community. Accordingly, an experimental halfway house is set up and a sample of inmates released into it. The inmates' behaviour is observed for, say, twelve or twenty-four months following release, and compared with the behaviour of similar inmates released directly into the community. Levels of adjustment to life outside prison—for example, rates of re-arrest and unemployment, levels of psychological well-being and social integration—are measured for the two groups and compared. If the group released into a halfway house does significantly better, the ministry may decide to extend this arrangement to larger numbers of released inmates. The demonstration project may also call attention to parts of the original plan that need fixing before the halfway house plan is adopted more widely.

Ideally, inmates will be randomly selected into the halfway house (the experimental condition) and the control group. Practical considerations may make a strict experimental design impossible; but the aim here is to learn from trial and error, not (as in the social-impact assessment) from speculation.

Evaluation studies. These examine demonstration projects and other programs to determine whether they have had the desired (predicted) effects, and if not, why not. Such studies are of two main types. *Process evaluation*, which often uses qualitative data (to be discussed in Chapter 4), determines whether the new arrangement — for example, the halfway house — worked as it was supposed to or ran into operating difficulties. *Outcome evaluation* determines whether the new arrangement produced the desired result: in this case, better-than-usual adjustment.

All three — social-impact assessment, demonstration project, and evaluation study — are predictive in the sense that they focus on the effects of a real or anticipated intervention. Recall that, using our terminology, every "predictive" study is characterized by one and only one independent variable — in this case, the intervention — and many dependent variables, or outcomes. The choice between a social-impact assessment and a demonstration project is largely guided by whether or not the intended intervention can reasonably be risked in the real world. Only a demonstration project can be evaluated, since only it produces real, not anticipated, results.

Explanatory studies

Explanatory studies aim to explain why something happens or happened. There is a dependent variable (or effect) that is to be explained by two or more independent variables (or causes). Most student papers, and many professional research projects, are of this type.

For example, you might wish to explain the amount of political violence in a society by examining the standard of living, the mobilization and popular acceptance of anti-establishment factions, or government responses to demands for reform. Or you might wish to explain the location of cities by examining the arrangement of transportation routes, the proximity to agricultural land, or other characteristics of the terrain (whether dry or marshy, flat or rocky, and so on.)

Attempting to explain a dependent variable with only one independent variable will generally produce unsatisfactory results, no matter how promising the independent variable selected. This is because most social effects are produced by the addition and interaction of many causes. Further, working with only one independent variable provides no basis for judging how *relatively* important that cause is in explaining the effect under study. You should therefore plan to include two or more promising independent variables in your explanation.

The social sciences differ somewhat in their adherence to this rule. Psychology and economics, for example, are much more likely to examine the effects of one independent variable at a time. The rule is much more applicable to the remaining social-science disciplines.

Applied explanatory studies

Explanatory design is also used in applied research, which is action- or policy-oriented. Three examples are the needs assessment, the market survey (or political poll), and the Royal Commission. The first two are used by a large variety of organizations; the third, only by government. Yet they share common features.

Needs assessments. These are explanatory studies that begin with a very thorough description of some social problem (e.g., problem-drinking) or social group (e.g., problem-drinkers), and aim to find out how widespread and how harmful the problem is. Such a study is called a "needs assessment" because it is an attempt to find out, or assess, whether a policy or program is needed to reduce the problem.

After describing the problem, the needs assessment typically theorizes about its causes and, ultimately, recommends whether or not the organization *should* take action, given the discovered extent of the problem, its likely causes, and the organizational resources for influencing these causes. Such a study usually precedes other types of research—namely, the demonstration project and the social-impact assessment—that focus attention on the interventions that are possible.

Market surveys and political polls. These are applied explanatory studies concerned with selling something to someone, be it a refrigerator to a homemaker, or a political candidate to a voter. In each instance the researcher is concerned with measuring the extent of support for the "product," the characteristics of respondents who are the strongest supporters or worst detractors, and the reasons for support and non-support.

The goal of such research is to modify marketing strategy to produce more effective sales (i.e., more support). This is done by (1) aiming sales more directly at those kinds of people revealed to be already most susceptible to the product; (2) changing the product, in fact or in appearance, to make it more appealing to its detractors; or (3) changing the sales pitch to make it capitalize more effectively on consumers' secret fears and wishes—their *real* reasons for support and non-support.

In some cases the research may reveal that consumer indifference or hostility is so great that the product cannot be marketed successfully by any method. If so, the product may be removed from sale (or candidacy).

Royal Commissions. Such commissions are commonly convened in Canada and the United Kingdom to study a social problem and find out what people think is causing it. (Similar government inquiries are conducted, under other names, in other countries.) The Royal Commission's Report differs from the smaller needs assessment in paying attention to public and expert opinion, and to public sentiment about the problem and its possible solution. In a sense, it is a "politicized" needs assessment, aimed as much at enhancing the government's image as at solving the problem. Important Royal Commissions in Canada have included the MacDonald Commission on the future of the Canadian economy, the Badgley Commission on the extent and causes of sexual child abuse, the LeDain Commission on the non-medical use of drugs, and the Kent Commission on the extent of monopoly ownership in the mass media. Each produced a great deal of descriptive research, theorized about the cause of present problems, and suggested legislation to deal with them.

EXERCISE 3

Applied explanation

Is the Canadian postal service slower and relatively more costly than many other postal services in the world, and if so, why?

1. Reword the question to identify the "causes" and the "effects."
2. Propose half a dozen possible explanations.

3. Which of your explanations could give rise to a govern-
    ment policy or program for solving the problems of the
    postal service?

Systemic studies

Systemic studies attempt to explain two or more effects by two or
more causes. Such studies are common in all the social sciences,
especially social history, ethnography, the field observation of groups,
and the analysis of organizations or governments. The subject under
study typically comprises many persons and many parts: it may be a
group, an organization, a community, or a society. The researcher's
ultimate goal is to understand how this system of interlinked parts
and persons works: how the parts affect one another, often in indirect,
reciprocal, and self-modifying ways.

Explaining the causes of the Second World War would require a
systemic study: for not only did the war have many causes, but what
we think of as the war—its outbreak, course, and conclusion—also
had many aspects (economic, diplomatic, military, and social), all
influencing one another and jointly "keeping the war alive".

An example on a smaller scale would be the analysis of a recently
computerized business organization. Computerization has many effects
on an organization: on procedure, profit-making, worker morale,
division of labour, and so on. But computerization is often accompanied or preceded by many other causes producing these effects: changes
in the *need* for profit-making, organizational rationality, the sym-
bolic demonstration of openness to change, and the availability of
money, personnel, hardware, and software for technological change.
To make sense of all the effects, it is necessary to understand all the
causes, of which computerization is only one.

A systemic design is often useful when you have started on an
explanatory design and found too many interlinked causes and effects
for a neat solution. Try shifting to a systemic design, and then focus
your attention on how these linkages maintain one another. (Some
might even argue that a systemic design is always appropriate if you
are explaining how or why something happens, since you are always
interested in knowing the reciprocal links among all the variables.)

EXERCISE 4

A question of design

What conditions tend to support and maintain totalitarian
government?

1. Restate this question: first, as it might be asked in a relational study; then, as in an explanatory study; then, as in a systemic study.
2. Would you get the same answers if the question were asked in these different ways? If not, how would the answers differ?

A good example of where systemic modelling may be useful is in the study of the "revolving door": the process by which skid-row alcoholics (or other "down-and-out" deviants) are repeatedly thrown into trouble with the law. What may begin as a simple drinking problem, unemployment, or homelessness is worsened by contact with the law. Once incarcerated, the deviant loses his or her self-respect, job, or family, and is worse off after incarceration than before it. It is then harder than ever to deal with the initial problem of drinking, homelessness, or unemployment; the likelihood of getting into more trouble and landing in jail is greater than ever. Finally, the deviant's chances of gaining any foothold in the "straight world" are lost entirely.

This example shows that a study that starts out as a simple analysis of problem-drinking (or unemployment, or trouble with the law) may end up dealing with the linkages among all of these variables that repeatedly support and intensify one another's effects.

CLOSING COMMENTS

To summarize, an *explanatory* study focuses attention on one *dependent* variable. It measures and compares the influence of many causes. A *predictive* study, on the other hand, focuses attention on one *independent* variable, and measures and compares the significance of many effects. The *relational* study is like neither of these: it focuses attention on *conditioning* variables that modify the effect of the independent on the dependent variable. It is a design that discovers and analyses important conditioning variables. Finally, the *systemic* study focuses attention on the interdependence of all causes and effects: on the system-like character of relationships. It is therefore concerned with analysing an entire *system* of independent, dependent, intervening and conditioning variables.

Don't mix designs

It should now be clear why, as a beginning researcher, you are wise to avoid mixing research designs. After all, different designs answer different questions, focus attention on different variables or relations between variables, and draw attention away from the rest.

Given too little time to do everything well, you should first and foremost attend to the central question, or issue, in your paper: to the dependent variable (in an explanatory study), the independent variable (in a predictive study), the most important conditioning variable(s) (in a relational study), and the relations among all variables (in a systemic study). If err you must, err on the side of saying too much about your central concern (e.g., about the independent variable in a predictive study) and too little about the rest.

There is one exception to this general rule: sometimes it is permissible to mix relational and explanatory designs. We shall say more about the usefulness of this strategy in the next chapter.

EXERCISE 5

A wide-open question

Why are addictions (to drugs, alcohol, tobacco) so difficult to cure?

1. Reword this question to identify the "causes" and the "effects."
2. Which of the four design types we have discussed here would be the most appropriate to answer this question, and which the least? Why?
3. How would your choice of design influence the kinds of information you would collect to answer the question?

Mixing designs is sensible if the researcher is aware of doing so; in this event, each design should be brought to a satisfactory completion. But the average student researcher has neither unlimited time or money, nor expertise in every kind of design; therefore modest goals are called for. Don't do more than you can do well. Choose one task— that is, one design—and see it through to completion. There is no need to apologize for what you haven't done if what you *have* done is excellent.

REFERENCES

Lipset, Seymour Martin

1963 *Political Man: The Social Bases of Politics*. Garden City, N.Y.: Anchor Books, Doubleday.

Lipset, Seymour Martin, Martin Trow, and James Coleman

1956 *Union Democracy: The Internal Politics of the International Typographical Union*. Garden City, N.Y.: Anchor Books, Doubleday.

3
Theory

A very large proportion of papers contain explanations. The process of explaining has two parts:

1. developing a theory, or theoretical model, to help the researcher think about relationships among the dependent and independent variables, and
2. collecting data, to test the correctness (validity) of that explanation.

What follows is an examination of the ways to ensure that your explanation will "make sense." Many points made below will apply just as readily to the predictive, systemic, and relational designs discussed in the last chapter. Also, bear in bind that these points will be just as useful in evaluating and criticizing other people's explanations as in constructing your own.

What is a good explanation?

A good explanation is persuasive, and it gets its persuasiveness from a number of features:

- It is logically consistent.
- Its component variables are clearly defined and well measured.
- It agrees with the observed data.
- It is parsimonious, in the sense that it requires us to make few untested assumptions or leaps of faith, and uses fewer independent variables than any other competing theory that explains the dependent variable no better.
- Most important, the causal (independent) variables are all temporally prior to the dependent variable— they can be shown to have happened first. (Remember, a cause cannot happen *after* its supposed effect.)

- Finally, a good explanation is better than any currently available alternative.

This chapter will introduce some basic concepts in theory-making: namely, the ideas of paradigm, theory, and prediction. You will be warned to keep aware of your main and secondary questions at all times, and to investigate their connection to both larger and smaller issues of theoretical importance. The chapter will end with a discussion of seven theoretical problems to avoid.

PARADIGMS

What paradigm are you following?

In every social science there are different "paradigms," or ways of thinking about the same question. They proceed from different basic assumptions about how the world works and give rise to different conclusions about important questions to ask and appropriate data to collect.

For example, two competing paradigms in sociology and anthropology (though not as distinct from one another as some have argued) are the structural-functionalist and Marxist/materialist/radical paradigms. The functionalist interprets criminal behaviour as evidence of inadequate upbringing, psychopathology, or membership in a deviant subgroup. The radical theorist, by contrast, interprets it as evidence of alienation, economic need, or protest against the ruling interests of society.

Each way of interpreting criminality leads a researcher to ask different questions, collect different kinds of data, and reach different conclusions. Nothing prevents you from collecting data that address *both* paradigms at the same time; in fact, this is a desirable practice. But social scientists often work in one paradigm at a time. (Some philosophers even believe that the advancement of scientific knowledge proceeds by this adversarial process.)

Know how your main question relates to larger questions

If your explanation draws more heavily on one paradigm than another, be sure of the assumptions you are making and the larger questions that your approach suggests. Collect data that would clearly connect your research to other research within the same paradigm.

For example, suppose you have found that most characters in television situation comedies are contented middle-class people. Few poor people or minority groups are portrayed at all, and when they are they appear weak, foolish, or immoral. This finding would tend to support the radical view that the mass media are tools used by the powerful to maintain the established order by spreading an illusion of general contentment, ridiculing the poor and/or discontented, and implying an unbridgeable gap between the interests of the middle class and others.

An argument along these lines would be strengthened by demonstrating that

1. other types of programs (e.g., the news, or soap operas) show a similar tendency;
2. such programming proceeds from "formulas" that are consciously created by media management with certain pro-establishment goals in mind; and
3. the media are owned and controlled by the economic or political elite.

Even if it is beyond the scope of your assignment to collect data relevant to these questions, you can at least raise the issues, to show your awareness that this research relates to larger questions within the same paradigm.

In making this connection, you should be aware of the problems usually associated with, or criticisms directed against, research within each paradigm. To continue our example, research claiming to show that television content demonstrates ideological manipulation by the ruling class should also be able to show that media manipulation has the desired effect on viewers. If not, how do we account for its continuation? And how would we deal with the argument that the media merely reflect viewer characteristics and beliefs, not mould them?

Once aware of the general and particular criticisms of your position, make sure you address them. Even if you cannot collect all the information needed to lay them to rest, at least show that you are aware of such criticisms and suggest further research that would deal adequately with them.

Don't play intellectual one-upmanship

As important as it is to locate your work within a paradigm, you shouldn't get carried away. Your real purpose is to answer a question, not to prove that some paradigm is better or worse than another. A paradigm will prove its usefulness by helping you answer the question at hand.

But the real world is very complicated. You may find that more than one paradigm contributes to your understanding of a particular problem. Many perspectives and, perhaps, many disciplines may contribute to a good answer. If so, acknowledge that fact even if it means using a paradigm you had not previously accepted. Theories are to be used by researchers, not researchers by theories. Denying the weaknesses in your own paradigm and the strengths in another, for partisan reasons, is bad research practice, mere intellectual one-upmanship. Findings and interpretations generated in this way will not hold up for very long and will do little to advance social science.

EXERCISE 6

Competing paradigms

Why may an act be a crime in one society but not in another?

1. Try answering this question first within the functional paradigm, and then within the radical paradigm.
2. What issues does each approach ignore?
3. Can the two answers—functionalist and radical—be integrated into a single answer, or are they incompatible?

THEORIES

The research cycle

The creation and testing of good theory proceeds through a research cycle, depicted in Figure 3.1. You begin with a *theory*: a set of logically related statements about some phenomenon of interest. From this theory you logically deduce hypotheses. *Hypotheses*, sometimes called *propositions*, are statements about presumed relationships between two or more variables. They give rise to specific predictions that are not known to be true, but that can be proved true or false, valid or invalid, by the collection and analysis of data.

For example, you might hypothesize about whether working mothers are more likely to experience guilt and anxiety than working fathers or non-working mothers. You start with the premise—suggested by your theory—that people are likely to experience guilt and anxiety if they are failing to meet their obligations or the expectations others have of them.

Figure 3.1
THE RESEARCH CYCLE

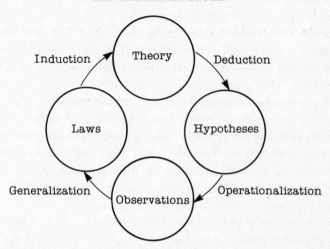

You may then premise that working fathers and non-working mothers traditionally each have only one major obligation (the fathers, their job; the non-working mothers, their household duties), while working mothers each have two major obligations (job and household duties). From this you may *deduce* the hypothesis that working mothers, with twice as many obligations, are twice as likely to fail to meet their obligations. This being so, they are twice as likely to experience guilt and anxiety in their lives.

Next comes the process of *operationalizing* the concepts in your hypothesis, so that you can verify it: that is, test it for truth or falsity. This process creates empirical measures of the key concepts (measurement will be discussed at length in the next two chapters). The measurement procedures produce *observations* that either support the hypothesis or prove it wrong. From these specific observations come *generalizations*: conclusions about the general significance of the observations for the hypothesis as originally stated.

The last stage of the cycle is *induction*, the process of reconciling the generalized results (or "laws") with the theory as originally stated. Where these two fail to fit together, a reformulation of the theory is called for. Then the cycle begins again, with another study and new hypotheses.

To follow up on the previous example, the empirical (i.e., observed or measured) data may reveal any of the following: (a) that working mothers are indeed found to be twice as guilty and anxious than either working fathers or non-working mothers; (b) that they are more than twice as guilty or anxious; or (c) that they are less guilty and anxious than working fathers and non-working mothers.

If result (a) is achieved the hypothesis is considered to have been supported or validated; accordingly, the theory that gave rise to the hypothesis is also considered validated. If result (b) or (c) is achieved, the hypothesis is not considered validated and, accordingly, neither is the theory that gave rise to it. However, result (b), being in the direction predicted (though not of the right magnitude), gives greater confidence in the general correctness of the theory than does (c). Result (b) would probably lead the researcher to look for reasons why observed guilt and anxiety proved greater than predicted (for example, reasons having to do with sampling or measurement, to be discussed later). Result (c) would less certainly lead in that direction, and might instead lead you to rethink your theory completely.

It is important to emphasize that no theory is ever proved finally and conclusively correct in this way (or any other!). We speak of a theory being proved true or false only as a shorthand to say that, for the time being, it is apparently more valid or true than any other theory about the same phenomenon. It may be proved invalid tomorrow by a better theory or a better test.

Thus all research produces at best tentative conclusions. Many believe that the purpose of research is to prove the best existing theory false, clearing the way for a better one. This should relieve any anxiety you might have about being wrong: researchers are often wrong—in the long run, almost always. But we can see their errors and inadequacies clearly only in hindsight.

Getting to know your own theory

The use of flow charts

Reaching a clear understanding of what you are arguing is more difficult than you might think, but following some easy steps will help. Start by listing all your variables. Then lay them out in a diagram connecting the variables influencing one another by labelled arrows, with a plus sign (+) indicating a positive relationship between two variables and a minus sign (−), a negative one. (Remember that in a positive relationship the connected variables increase and decrease together, while in a negative relationship one variable increases as the other decreases.) Some pairs of variables may not be connected at all.

Diagramming an explanation forces you to deal consciously with what you think is going on: what are the key variables; what are the important relationships and non-relationships; what parts of the overall model can reasonably be analysed separately from one another; and, therefore, how you must analyse the data to test your theory.

A typical explanatory diagram or *flow chart*, as it is sometimes called, displays the dependent variable on the right hand side and the independent variables on the left. Thus the order of supposed causation flows from left to right, through intervening variables that come into effect after (or occasionally at the same time as) the independent variables. One version of such a flow chart, called a *path model*, is depicted in Figure 3.2.

This path model (simplified for use here) is a standard diagram used by sociologists to illustrate the relationship between a son's occupation and income and the characteristics of his class of origin (or father's occupation and income). It is generally called the "status-attainment model." Containing results from a study done in Ontario, it shows that father's occupation has no direct effect on the occupation of his son (the "respondent") once the son's education is taken into account. But father's occupation *does* have an important direct effect on how much education the son will get, and hence an important indirect effect on son's occupation. Note also the important direct effects of unmeasured variables on son's occupation. They show that sociologists are far from knowing the full causes of occupational attainment. (The particular numbers in the diagram, called *path coefficients*, range between 0, meaning no effect, and ±1, meaning a very strong positive or negative effect.)

Figure 3.2
A simplified path diagram of the
stratification process: Ontario, 1978

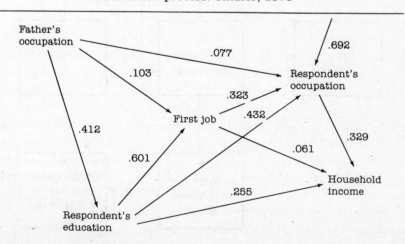

The same left-to-right convention cannot be used in depicting a systemic model. Here many independent and dependent variables affect one another at the same time, even feeding back on one another repeatedly. One such model is shown in Figure 3.3, which aims at explaining why pre-industrial populations tend to keep returning to a particular size. Try tracing through the argument it charts.

The "positive" and "preventive" checks noted by the demographer Thomas Malthus are both in evidence here. As population size increases, the size of an average landholding decreases, mortality rises, and the population size falls back to its earlier level. This is the positive check. Also, as population size increases, the supply of labour increases; real income per head decreases; people marry later (or not at all); community fertility or child-bearing declines; and the population size falls back to its earlier level. This is the preventive check, "preventive" in the sense that a rise in the death rate is prevented.

Figure 3.3
A model of relationships between demographic, social
and economic change in a pre-industrial society

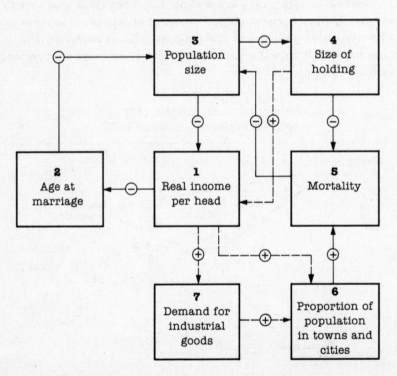

Figure 3.4, another systemic model, follows a slightly different convention. In this model of organizational functioning, the first dependent variable, "demand for control," is presented at the top of the chart, and later effects are presented below it in descending order of their occurrence.

The model, derived from Gouldner's *Patterns of Industrial Bureaucracy* (1954), shows how a demand to exercise more managerial control over workers by means of general and impersonal (i.e., bureaucratic) rules has the final effect of increasing interpersonal tensions and creating a need for even more rules than before. This helps to explain why bureaucracies produce ever more rules (and, it seems, ever more tension within the work organization).

Figure 3.4

The simplified Gouldner model

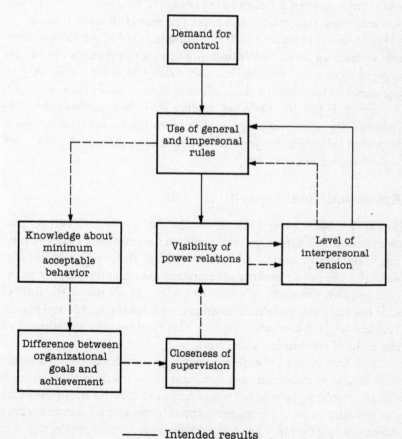

EXERCISE 7

Flow charts

How do course grades affect students' educational plans
and career aspirations?

1. What design is most appropriate for answering this
   question?
2. What are the key variables in your answer?
3. Use a flow chart to diagram all positive and negative
   relations among the key variables.

Get a friend to help you theorize

Knowing your own theory is, as we have seen, not so easy. That is why
you sometimes need a disinterested person to help you remember why
you are doing this project and what you expect to learn from it.

Find a friend or relative with five minutes to spare, preferably someone without social-science training. Then try to explain what you are
arguing about and why. If you can make the main pieces of your
argument fit together for this audience, you probably know what you
are doing. If you have trouble making sense to your listener—or to
yourself—try again, with the same or (even better) another audience.
Repeated failures to make sense in this setting suggest that all is not
well with your explanation.

Know your main question

So far we have been looking at the big picture: locating your
explanation in a larger body of research and ensuring that you have
taken account of all the relevant variables. But we should not lose
sight of a key point: making sense means always knowing your prime
goal or main question. It's easy to get lost in all the particulars of
your research: the variables, measures, and debates (great and small).
People who have been working long and hard on some question often
lose sight of the forest for the trees.

Sometimes losing sight of your main goal comes about in another
way. You may chance into a "treasure trove" of data that are only
slightly related to the original research question. If you start ransacking
this treasure of data for nuggets (there is no end to the interesting
things you can find in a good library or survey, or even in the reported
census results), after a while you may forget to use the data to answer

the original question, and simply report on all the data instead.

The sociologist C. Wright Mills (1959:Chap. 3) called this failure "abstracted empiricism." It is research "abstracted" or removed not only from the great questions of social life (which is what primarily concerned Mills), but even from the smaller questions the research was originally intended to answer. The researcher has left an explanatory design for description or exploration.

Suppose that you started out with a theory that people's job satisfaction is primarily influenced by social relations on the job. You discover a survey of job satisfaction that someone else has done, primarily examining the effect of working conditions and economic incentives, but including one question on how well people relate to their work-mates. The data reveal all sorts of interesting relationships, but only a weak relationship between job satisfaction and workers' relations with their work-mates. Does this finding disprove your original theory? No: in this report the data are quite irrelevant. Instead of measuring the key explanatory variable, social relations on the job, in a variety of useful ways, you have measured it in only one way, which may be flawed or irrelevant. Mainly, you have redirected attention to a number of other possible explanations about which you have no theory. Exploration is not bad in itself; but you should be aware if you have changed designs in this way. You cannot automatically move back from an unstructured exploration into an effective explanation.

If you have done this, your three choices are clear: rethink your goal and admit it is an exploration, not an explanation, of the dependent variable; or find another body of data that better measures social relations on the job; or develop some theories about the likely role of working conditions and economic incentives, about which you have plenty of data.

Know how your main question relates to secondary questions

You can never go too far in thinking about your main question of interest and secondary, related questions. These related questions should be addressed with data if possible, or at least acknowledged as deserving later research. Examples might include explanations of why particular intervening or contextual factors are important, or discussions of paradigm-related issues.

Imagine, for example, that research on situation comedies had found that the central characters were always middle-class people living a prosperous, urban life-style, and that this portrayal implied to viewers that such a life-style was desirable, easily obtainable, and a reward for social conformity.

You might then analyse the component parts of this portrayal. What does it mean that people in these stories hold certain kinds of jobs, wear certain kinds of clothes, or have certain kinds of furniture? That is, what meanings do viewers attach to certain roles or material objects in our environment, and where do these meanings come from? Why, for example, are doctors almost invariably portrayed as heroic, unselfish, and helpful? What is the social meaning of "doctor" in our culture, how did it arise, and how is it maintained despite our first-hand experience that doctors, like everyone else, are often quite unheroic, selfish, and unhelpful?

EXERCISE 8

Primary and secondary questions

What managerial practices are most likely to increase worker morale and productivity?

1. Are worker morale and productivity related, and if so, how?
2. What managerial practices are likely to influence each? And how do morale and productivity influence managerial practices?
3. What design is most useful in answering this question? Make a flow chart to help answer it.

Explore at different levels of analysis

The social sciences involve research at several different levels of analysis, as the examples in this book suggest. Social scientists study societies, organizations, communities, and individuals—social formations characterized by different levels or degrees of complexity. Two points should be made about levels of analysis.

Avoid reductionism

Although some important theorists have argued to the contrary, problems at one level of analysis cannot be easily broken down, or reduced, to a larger number of smaller problems at a lower level of analysis. Such a strategy, called *reductionism*, is not acceptable in most cases. Take the example of social-movement formation: why people join together to protest economic, religious, or some other type of discrimination or inequality. This question cannot be answered simply by moving down to the individual level of analysis and studying the psychology—the attitudes and motives—of participating protesters.

That is because a sense of outrage may be *necessary* for a social movement to form, but it is far from *sufficient*. For protest to actually occur, the outraged people must mobilize: there must be leadership, communication, a shared consciousness, and often material facilities—money, food, cars, bombs, other types of expertise in protesting. For this reason the rise of a protest movement does not prove that people have just become outraged: they may have just mobilized. Likewise, the absence of protest does not prove people are not outraged, but may prove that they are not organized.

This example shows that a social phenomenon can—and often must—be examined at various levels of analysis simultaneously if we are to understand it fully. We may discover that forces operating at different levels of analysis are pulling in opposite directions. For example, at the individual level people may feel outraged at their own and other people's unemployment. Yet unemployed people tend to be politically inactive: they do not protest their condition to demand a remedy. Part of this problem is "organizational" as we have just described it: a shortage of leaders, resources, and communication.

But part of it is cultural. Our value system holds people responsible for their own fate. People in Canada are brought up to believe that what happens to them is their own fault: they have earned their successes and failures and must live with them. Thus on the psychological level all the conditions may be met for social action against unemployment, while on the cultural level the opposite conditions prevail. Along with problems at the social-organizational level, cultural (or ideological) factors work against the behavioural expression of forces operating at the psychological, or individual level.

Test theories at all levels of analysis

To say that theories should be tested at all levels of analysis may seem to contradict what we have just said about opposing forces at different levels; and indeed analyses at different levels will often give different results. But this is not always the case.

Consider the issue of punitiveness. Societies vary in their degree of punitiveness: that is, in how severely they punish wrongdoers. Canada is visibly much less punitive than many societies, in the sense that here people are not banished, tortured or executed for minor (or even major) offences, as is the case in other societies (and has historically been so). Yet Canada does imprison a higher proportion of convicted criminals than many other modern nations. What accounts for Canada's position as a punitive country relative to many others?

We might hypothesize that this punitiveness is the result of internal instability: societies (and also groups, communities, and individuals) that "feel" insecure are more likely to punish severely, in order to increase their internal cohesion by reaffirming moral boundaries.

At what level should this hypothesis be tested? The answer is that it can, and perhaps should, be tested at all levels of analysis. If the hypothesis is valid, we should find that individuals who are most socially or economically marginal or insecure will express the most punitive sentiments towards wrongdoers. At the societal level, rates of punitiveness (i.e., rates of imprisonment for convicted criminals) should increase in times of war, economic depression, or internal unrest, in response to perceived threats to the society. At the cultural level, racism, nationalism, xenophobia and other declarations of preference for people like oneself should, along with punitiveness, increase when the culture is being threatened by massive immigration or foreign domination of the mass media.

If we find that all of these changes do occur as predicted, there is reason to believe we have found the basis for a general theory of punitiveness. Our work is far from done, however. Without examining the process by which punitiveness is increased at each level under conditions of internal instability, we run the risk of two grave methodological errors, both connected with improper movement between levels of analysis: the ecological fallacy and the fallacy of misplaced concreteness (for a detailed discussion of these, see pp. 41-2). But if these fallacies can be avoided, our multi-level theory will be more compelling than a theory that holds good at only one level of analysis.

PREDICTIONS

Know what new ideas or predictions your theory suggests

The essential purpose of a theory is to explain, or clarify, how variables are related to one another. One way to test a theory's validity is to make predictions based on the model and to test them with data.

Prediction is not the only test of a theory, for several reasons. Certain theories cannot be immediately tested with data—some of Einstein's theories in physics waited decades for testing, until the appropriate technology was available. As well, a theory-based explanation that may be generally correct may fail to yield valid predictions because of faulty measures, incomplete data, or unrecognized intervening or contextual factors.

Conversely, good predictions can be made even without a good, highly developed theory. For example, traffic engineers can accurately predict the flow of traffic past a particular intersection for a given day or week. They base their prediction on many past observations, not on a theory about traffic. This kind of predicting uses what is sometimes called a *black-box* approach. It can effectively use data to make predictions, but what happens in between, in the "black box" where causes produce effects, is largely unknown. For many practical purposes, it need not be known.

As well, predictions based on historical explanations are rarely testable. An explanation or theory about the causes of the Russian Revolution cannot do better than persuade the reader through its logical, plausible handling of already existing information. In this instance, attempts may be made to verify the theory by a comparison with other revolutions—that is, by developing a general theory of revolutions—but this enterprise is rather different and full of problems of comparability among societies.

But if prediction is not the ultimate test of an explanation, it is nonetheless desirable. Social science is often accused of merely restating the obvious in difficult jargon. To get past this criticism, researchers should aim to show that their theories can produce ideas, understanding, or findings that are not possible using common sense alone.

Consider the question of how families deal with the stresses produced by chronic illness. Common sense tells us that families will deal with their difficulties in different ways—a true prediction, but vague. Systematic observation and theory show us *which* families cope better than others and *which* coping strategies work better than others. They show that adjustment proceeds through a series of stages, each with its own problems and resolutions, before the next stage can be attempted. If we are trying to understand why a particular family is coping in the way it is and how it can be helped to cope better, we are far better off with a theory to help us than with common sense alone. With theory we can hope not only to predict the future course of a family's problems, but also to predict which interventions will work best at given times, for a given family.

EXERCISE 9

The value of theory

The decision to have a baby is very much like the decision to buy a "consumer durable" (e.g., a house, car, or refrigerator).

1. How does this comparison of child-bearing with major purchases help us predict child-bearing? (Hint: Start by considering how the two decisions are similar, then review the factors that appear to influence the purchase of consumer durables. Do they also seem likely, on logical grounds, to influence child-bearing?)
2. How does this comparison help us predict the purchase of consumer durables?

State your expectations before you do the analysis

Creating a flow chart is the best way of "stating your expectations," but it is not the only one. Even without a flow chart, you should be explicit about what you expect the data to reveal and why. This will help to clarify your theoretical assumptions, suggest appropriate research methodology needed to test your theory, and point to missing variables that might explain or interpret your result.

Anticipating your findings means you win whichever way the data turn out when you analyse them. If the expected result occurs, you can reasonably claim that this supports your theory, since that theory was able to make the correct prediction. If, on the other hand, unexpected results show up, the analysis becomes even more interesting. Many useful findings in social science are overlooked because they show no relationship where one had been expected; or a negative relationship where a positive one had been expected; or a weak relationship where a strong one had been expected.

If you have developed your theory carefully, linking your explanation to questions and findings in the literature, you are right to have expected what you did. The fact that your result is unexpected points to a need for rethinking, or for considering additional variables you and others have overlooked; it may even mean that your entire line of argument is wrong.

Moving into a relational design

When unexpected results occur, your analysis should move out of an explanatory design into a relational one. The search is on for intervening variables that make sense of the observed unexpected relationship between the independent and dependent variables. A deviant-case analysis may be in order, for example.

Suppose you had predicted that, in a particular election, working-class people would vote for one party and middle-class people for another, because different parties protect different class interests. The results show something quite different: large numbers of working-class people voted for the "middle-class" party. Your theory of "class voting" may indeed be wrong, but other key variables may also play a part in making the theory generally correct. For example, working-class voters may have *believed* that the "middle-class party" would protect working-class interests. If so, you should modify, not discard, your original theory of class voting. We find that people will vote for their class interests as *they perceive* them, and as *they perceive* the platform of the party they are voting for. In this way you are led to focus on a new, interesting problem of political misinformation or manipulation and to collect new data on people's perceptions not considered previously.

Know the conditions under which you expect your theory to hold true

All explanatory studies contain elements of a relational design. None can rightly ignore the context within which the data are collected, nor the factors likely to make the explanation stronger or weaker.

The most obvious examples are the historical and cultural contexts. Every social fact and social law holds true in a particular time and place. Showing that something is universal and timeless requires a great deal of data. The fact that in one factory social relations on the job do exercise an important influence on job satisfaction cannot automatically be generalized to all factories. This relationship may be stronger in unionized than non-unionized factories, where concerns about job security, working conditions, or pay are greater. It may be stronger in a period of prosperity than in one of mass unemployment, for similar reasons. And it may be stronger in small-scale, traditional workplaces, or in newly industrializing societies, than in modern, highly bureaucratized or mechanized workplaces located in industrialized societies.

Specifying the conditions under which your theory holds true is important in several ways. First, it helps you clarify what is going on and why. Second, it helps you and others judge the generality of your findings and their applicability to other situations.

Generalizability is sometimes particularly important in applied research, where decisions affecting others are based on research findings. Imagine a demonstration project to determine how citizen/police relations might be improved in a particular city. Someone theorizes that such relations are improved by an easier, less formal availability of policemen to citizen enquiries. On this basis, the theorist suggests taking some police out of their centralized police station and putting them into a storefront "mini-station," where people can come to ask questions, lodge complaints, and mix with policemen in a relaxed way. Such a mini-station is set up for a trial period of six months, and then community members are surveyed to determine whether their views of the police have improved. The data show no change in views.

What conclusion can be drawn from this finding? Further, should the experiment be continued or even extended to other neighbourhoods? Our answer depends in large part on the characteristics of the neighbourhood in which the mini-station was situated: for example, on whether the community members had originally been very fearful of the police, had tended to misinterpret their motives and behaviours, and felt reluctant to make initial, let alone subsequent, contacts. The results have a very different meaning if found in an unreceptive community than in a receptive one.

EXERCISE 10

Contextual factors

Why are Canadians not highly class-conscious?

1. Answer this question as originally stated.
2. Now, consider under what historical, political, or economic conditions Canadians are more and less likely to be class-conscious. At any given time, which Canadians are more likely, and which less likely, to be class-conscious?
3. Do the differences in class-consciousness among Canadians suggest differences between Canada and other countries? If so, what differences?
4. Given your answer above, which countries would you predict to be more or less class-conscious than Canada?

PITFALLS TO AVOID

The process of making and testing theory is full of pitfalls. Some are so common as to have become "classic" social-science problems with names to identify them. Social scientists have spent a great deal of time discussing these pitfalls, and you can read more about them in the literature. What follows is a brief account of seven such problems, which you should avoid.

The ecological fallacy

The ecological fallacy is the mistake of drawing a conclusion at one level of analysis and applying it to another. Social science analyses data at several different levels of complexity: those of the individual person, the group, the institution, the society, and the culture. Moving between levels of analysis can lead to errors.

For example, imagine that research has found that delinquency rates are highest in those parts of a city where average household income is lowest. This does *not* necessarily prove that low-income *children* are more often delinquent than higher-income children. High-income children may be the delinquents in both parts of town, but in the wealthier parts delinquency by high-income children may less often result in detection, arrest, or conviction.

Likewise, we are not justified in doing what Emile Durkheim (1951) did in his classic study of suicide. He studied suicide rates for a variety of countries and, noting that the rates were higher in countries that were predominantly Protestant, inferred that Protestants were more suicide-prone than Catholics. However, he did so without any direct evidence that Protestants, not Catholics, were committing the suicides in question.

To repeat, we are never justified in inferring individual behaviour from ecological or aggregate data (i.e., rates of behaviour in entire neighbourhoods, cities, or nations). Aggregate data merely *suggest* relationships that can be tested with other data. They may also be used, in some cases, to explain other aggregate data.

Multicollinearity

Often many independent variables are highly correlated with one another; that is, they vary together. This phenomenon is known as multicollinearity. Consider the problem of explaining the dramatic decline in average family size (or married child-bearing) observed throughout the Western world in the late nineteenth and early twentieth centuries. The decline is correlated with a great many changes that are also correlated with one another: the spread of literacy, urbanization, industrialization, increased standard of living, reduced child mortality, and so on. All of these variables tended to change together (and to change one another), which is why they are often lumped together under the general term "modernization." To say which of these was the key influence on child-bearing is extremely difficult, almost arbitrary. It is therefore quite arbitrary which one we identify as being *most* important in producing the observed effect. As a researcher, then, you should avoid making any strong claims about the causal influence of a particular variable in such a situation.

EXERCISE 11

Multicollinearity

What social values are most important in promoting economic productivity?

1. Reword this question to identify the "causes" and the "effects."
2. Propose a half-dozen possible answers to this question.
3. Which of the factors you named above are related to one another, and how are they related? That is, what are the connections among the causes you have identified?

The fallacy of misplaced concreteness

You commit the fallacy of misplaced concreteness if you attribute to some abstract entity (e.g., the society or the community) thoughts or behaviours of which only individual humans are capable. Like the ecological fallacy, this mistake results from a confusion about levels of analysis.

So, for example, to characterize some societies as more warlike or militaristic than others is both implausible and imprecise. Societies do not make wars: people do. "Society" is an abstract or theoretical concept, and therefore incapable of acting. When we say that a society is warlike we are implying that all its people like wars, or that its major institutions or dominant classes are filled with people who are itching for a fight. More likely than not, however, a relatively small number of people are promoting military activity, and often for practical reasons (profit-making, broadening their power, increasing their prestige), not because they like war for its own sake.

Thus misplaced concreteness combines several grievous errors. First, it attributes actions and motives in a sloppy, overly general way. It reduces social structure to individual traits, as though each member of society were identical and a miniature version of the entire society. It fails, in this instance, to identify who is militaristic and why; and further, why these people are often successful in causing wars. Second, this imprecision leads us away from an analysis of distinct conflicting individuals, groups, and classes, towards a nearly mystical belief in an acting, consensual society.

Tautology or circularity

Relationships that are true by definition are not worth researching since they tell us nothing new and cannot be falsified by data. Investigating such tautological, or circular, relationships adds nothing to our understanding.

For example, the theory that criminal behaviour results from social maladjustment, character disorder, or undersocialization is tautological if all we mean by these terms is a propensity to criminal behaviour. (Or, just as bad, we may think that maladjustment, character disorder, or undersocialization mean something more than mere criminal behaviour, but we cannot measure what this "something more" consists of.)

Such obvious tautology is rare; other kinds are more common. Consider the sociological theory of status attainment that says that in modern societies people's adult job status will be determined primarily by their educational attainment, whatever class they are born into. This theory proves largely tautological when we discover that "job status" here is measured in part by the average educational attainment of people in a particular job. Thus the theory states, "The attainment of a high-status job (that is, a job with a high average educational requirement) will be accomplished by obtaining a high level of education." This is tautology.

Unprovables

Theorizing about things you cannot measure — unprovables — will be useful under very few circumstances. Acknowledge at the outset if you are exploring or speculating about a topic, and not really theorizing. Of course, you may have a very tight, well-defined theory that can yield predictions well in advance of the technology to test them. Mathematical theories in physics have these properties, but such theories are rare in social science.

For the most part, therefore, you should stay away from theorizing about variables you cannot measure, since there is no way of telling whether you are right or wrong. This problem is worsened if your theory contains "escape clauses" to explain away results that are opposite to what you had predicted.

Consider two classic examples: Marx's theory of alienation, and Freud's theory of repression. Marx (1961) argues that, in a capitalist society, workers lack control over the labour process: over what will be made, how, and to whom the profits will flow. The result is a sense of alienation or estrangement from work, the product of work, oneself, and others. This gives rise to the prediction that, as we vary worker control, the expressed sense of alienation should vary. Yet studies have shown that many workers in (objectively) alienating work settings do not feel (subjectively) alienated. That is, they do not express feelings of estrangement from themselves, others, and so on. A Marxist would counter that such workers demonstrate a "false consciousness" (that is, a false perception of the class situation) that causes them to deny their true feelings. Since we cannot discover their "true feelings," we must conclude that this theory is unprovable, at least at present.

Freud's theory of repression is similar in many ways. He argues (1963) that people have certain natural or inborn drives: for example, drives toward the expression of sexual or aggressive impulses. However, the free expression of these drives is prevented or repressed in most societies, especially strongly in some. The theory would seem to predict that people will "sublimate," or redirect these impulses in "safe" directions (i.e., in ways that would not result in punishment); express the impulses in fantasy (e.g., dreams, art); or suffer neurotic symptoms if they do not express the impulses at all. However, many people demonstrate low levels of sexual or aggressive impulse in any form and yet do not appear neurotic.

A theorist from a contending school of psychology would say that the existence of these exceptions proves Freud wrong: that aggression and sexuality are learned, not instinctive, and that low levels of such expression are proof of learning (e.g., imitation and reward), not repression. A Freudian would respond that the apparent absence of expression shows denial or reaction formation, and that the instinctive impulses find their outlet in some other way — in smoking, overeating, loud laughter, or a strong devotion to work. But the Freudian theory is unprovable as it stands, since it contains no limit on the number of possible exceptions to the rule.

Constants

Constants are, as their name suggests, unchanging: they never vary. Thus a constant can never be used to explain anything; only variables can explain one another. More bluntly, no one can explain a variable by a constant, nor a constant by a variable, nor a constant by a constant. A constant just *is*.

Although the uselessness of constants in explanation should be obvious, unfortunately they enter into many explanations nonetheless. A prime example is the use of "human nature" to explain things, whether wars, divorces, discrimination, or the production of art. The statement "Wars are caused by human nature" is untestable as it stands. It would seem likely, at first glance, that data could refute this statement, since wars come and go, yet human nature presumably remains constant. However, someone might respond that wars are caused by a combination of human nature and some other factor (e.g., a shortage of agricultural land, resulting in population pressure). In this event, the researcher might just as well treat the other (variable) factor as the true explanation and ignore human nature.

Non-events

Non-events didn't happen. Yet researchers try to study them all the time. They try to study why released prisoners don't go straight; why countries didn't have revolutions; why cities aren't situated in particular places.

There are two reasons why you should be very cautious in studying non-events. One is that there are no data, since nothing happened. If it is true that people didn't evolve to look like ostriches, we would appear to have little to say about the conditions under which they would or could evolve to look like ostriches. Likewise, if Canada has never had a revolution, we can say little about the circumstances under which it would or could have one, except under conditions we shall specify shortly.

You are in a slightly better position to explain why things *did* happen, since there *are* data that can be plausibly arranged in an explanation. Take the example of a recent study by Peters and Waterman (1984) of "excellent" business organizations, which had the aim of explaining how excellence was achieved. The excellent organizations were examined in detail to find common features that logically might have contributed to their "excellence" (defined by the researchers as continued massive profitability).

Researchers find that these organizations all paid a lot of attention to client satisfaction, enjoyed great employee loyalty, and were highly specialized in a particular kind of product. One can imagine why client satisfaction, employee loyalty, and considerable expertise in one particular line *might* bring about success, or "excellence."

However, even this study of actual events is logically flawed. And this is the second reason for caution. By studying only one side of the equation—that is, only successes, and not failures as well—you run the risk of thinking that effects are causes, or that *sufficient* causes are *necessary* ones. In this particular case, attention to client satisfaction, employee loyalty, and product specialization may not have *caused* the success, but rather *resulted* from success. Successful organizations are more able to induce employee satisfaction, give attention to client satisfaction, and put all their efforts into (highly risky) specialization in one product than less successful, financially troubled organizations.

As well, none of these factors may be *necessary* to business success, or "excellence." Many businesses that do none of the above survive and prosper. For example, banks, insurance companies, utilities (such as the telephone company), and, most of all, government organizations do relatively little to ensure client satisfaction, employee loyalty, or expertise in a narrow range of activities. They don't need to, since they enjoy a monopoly over services. Legislation and other restrictions on competition (e.g., market dominance) ensure their profitable survival regardless of organizational adequacy—to use a slightly modified cliché, "monopoly" means never having to say "I'm sorry." Each of the immense "excellent" organizations the researchers studied may have prospered through market dominance and political support, not by virtue of the qualities the researchers identified.

The only way to be sure if a supposed cause is a necessary cause and not an effect, or a merely sufficient cause, or not a cause at all, is by means of *comparison*. Successes must be compared with failures, to see what factors are always present in the successes and always absent in the failures. More generally, non-events must always be compared with events, to see what factors are present in the one case and absent in the other.

Failing that, non-events must be studied in relation to a general theory about events (and non-events). For example, understanding why Canada hasn't had a revolution requires starting with a general theory of revolutions: a theory about the conditions needed to produce one. Making such a theory requires, as we have already noted, an investigation of both revolutionary and non-revolutionary societies: a comparison of non-revolutionary Canada with revolutionary Russia, France, or the United States, for example.

Our conclusion is that you should not study a non-event for purposes of explanation without either (a) a general theory about corresponding events, or (b) data on corresponding events.

EXERCISE 12

Some things to avoid

Canada has passed from being a colony of Britain to being a colony of the United States without ever having been a nation.

1. What are the key concepts in this statement?
2. Define the key concepts to make the statement verifiable.
3. Draw a flow chart to illustrate the argument.
4. What facts would you need to verify this statement?
5. Of which other nations might the same statement be made?

Non-findings

We stated earlier that the unexpected discovery of a non-finding may be cause for rejoicing. If a predicted result fails to appear, this may motivate the researcher to refine a theory, not discard it. However, consider again Figure 3.2 (p. 29), which explored the relationships between father's occupation, respondent's education, first job, occupation, and household income; it showed that all of the effects on respondent's occupation and income were relatively small: that is, closer to zero than to $+1$. Further, taking all these independent variables together left a large amount of uncertainty. The effect of unmeasured variables on occupation and income was twice as large as the effect of any measured variable. We have not *really* found out what is influencing respondent's occupation and income using this model. In this sense we have produced a non-finding. What conclusion should we draw?

One possibility is that a bad theory has led the researcher to measure the wrong variables. If so, the initial theory should have been rejected as unhelpful. Another is that the researcher has failed to take into account contextual or intervening factors; and that a good explanation will have to be much more complex than originally thought. Instead of adding together in some simple way, the various influences may interact or multiply together in any of what might be thousands of different ways. Such a conclusion, while conceivably the right one, must in the short run lead to despair. No one is able to investigate thousands of possible combinations among dozens or hundreds of independent variables. The researcher is, in effect, reduced to starting all over—making a new, simple theory—or giving up the problem altogether.

A third "solution" was suggested by Christopher Jencks (1972) in his analysis of social inequality. Jencks recognized that a vast number of status-attainment studies had been unable to predict job or income attainment very effectively. While such factors as class of birth, educational attainment, gender, and measures of ability had all contributed somewhat to the final result—a good job with a good income—a large area of unpredictability remained even when all the variables were considered together. As in Figure 3.2 (p. 29), the amount of unpredictability was larger than the amount of predictability. Jencks ascribed this unpredictability to an unmeasured and so far unmeasurable factor that he called "luck." Some people are simply luckier than others: they find themselves in the right place at the right time.

His theory has the appeal of common sense and everyday experience, but it does suffer from a deficiency discussed earlier: namely, the unmeasurability of the key variable "luck." Until we can measure luck, our understanding of its true role in people's lives is no better than speculation. As well, relabelling what is unknown as "luck" is not itself explanation.

Therefore the final, and perhaps the best, explanation of a non-finding—and its most dangerous meaning—is that one or more key variables have not been measured correctly. The researcher has not managed to predict "status attainment" either because he or she didn't really know what the term was supposed to mean; or because what the researcher meant was not what other people mean; or, finally, because the questions asked of respondents were badly worded or essentially irrelevant.

If so, the theory may be right or wrong, and there is no way of telling from the data available. We have been defeated by bad measurement.

CLOSING COMMENTS

This chapter has discussed the research cycle and the importance of clarity about the purposes of the research. We have examined paradigms, theories, and predictions—the analytical framework of any research undertaking. If you are unclear about what you are trying to prove, you cannot hope that anyone else will be clear about what you have found out. The result will be nonsense.

We have also examined seven classic problems of logical organization. Avoiding them will help you launch your research towards findings that will make sense. Yet still our job is only half done. We have our hypotheses in hand, but we have yet to measure the key variables in ways that will produce conclusive findings. This is the subject of the next chapter.

REFERENCES

Durkheim, Emile

    1951   *Suicide: A Study in Sociology*. Translated by John A. Spaulding and George Simpson. New York: Free Press of Glencoe.

Freud, Sigmund

    1963   *Civilization and Its Discontents*. Translated by Joan Riviere. London: Hogarth Press.

Gouldner, Alvin W.

    1954   *Patterns of Industrial Bureaucracy*. New York: Free Press of Glencoe.

Jencks, Christopher

    1972   *Inequality: A Reassessment of the Effect of Family and Schooling in America*. New York: Basic Books.

Marx, Karl.

    1961   *Economic and Philosophical Manuscripts of 1844*. Moscow: Foreign Languages Publishing House.

Mills, C. Wright

    1959   *The Sociological Imagination*. London: Oxford University Press.

Peters, Thomas J. and Robert H. Waterman Jr.

    1984   *In Search of Excellence: Lessons from America's Best Run Companies*. New York: Warner Books.

4
Measurement I:
obtaining data

As we have just seen, a project that starts out as good research, with good design and good theory, can be ruined by bad data. "Bad" data are either irrelevant to the question asked, or relevant but badly measured. How to measure data so that they directly address a theory or explanation is the subject of the next two chapters.

Much of the work you will do as a student will involve taking measurements from existing research studies and using them in your own research paper. Doing this well requires that you understand the basis of good measurement. Only with such an understanding will you be able to judge which data are trustworthy (and worth using) and which are not. As in earlier chapters, we will proceed as though you were starting from scratch to design and execute your own study. And here, too, you should keep in mind that it is just as important to apply these principles to the work of other researchers as it is to apply them to your own.

This chapter will touch lightly on a variety of important topics concerning measurement and data collection. Since each has been the subject of much debate and scholarly writing, we recommend that you pursue them further in a course on research methods.

We begin by discussing the process of "operationalization," that part of the research cycle in which the researcher proceeds from hypothesis to data collection. Operationalization requires a clear idea of the meaning of the concepts used and the hypotheses to be tested; these should determine the data to be collected. A brief discussion of two types of data, quantitative and qualitative, follows. (Again, our purpose here is only to familiarize you with some of the terms and concerns of the social scientist, not to provide a thorough grounding for empirical work.) The critical process of assessing the validity of the data collected, whether by you or by another researcher, is examined in the following chapter.

Suiting data to your theory

Suiting your data to your theory means doing two things. First, make sure that every variable in your hypothesis is measured by at least one set of data. For example, to test the explanation that a tolerance of free speech on controversial matters is determined by age, education, and an overall awareness of political issues, you must collect at least four pieces of information from each respondent: his/her age, educational attainment, stated level of political awareness, and, of course, stated tolerance of free speech.

Second, make sure to collect no more data than you need to test the theory. This rule can be relaxed as you become more experienced in research. For the newcomer, however, collecting too many data presents two major dangers: it increases the time and other costs of the study, and it threatens to divert attention from the key variables. If costs mount and attention is diverted, you may give too little attention to collecting good measures of your key variables. It's far better to collect two or three measures of each key variable, and few additional pieces of information, than to collect one measure for each of many variables that are less significant for the theory. The reason will become clear in due course.

Types and levels of measurement

As already noted, social scientists work with two types of measured data: quantitative and qualitative. Quantitative data are data to which number values can be assigned; qualitative data are those to which such values cannot be. Some researchers regard qualitative data as a poor approximation to quantitative data, indicating a low level of understanding of the phenomenon under study. Others, however, regard qualitative data as capturing more fully and accurately the "meaning" of observed phenomena than do numerical measurements that have been forced onto reality like a too-tight shoe.

On the one hand, it is clearly inadequate to say that Jack is taller than John if we can accurately measure the difference with a number scale showing that Jack is 200 centimetres tall and John is only 175 centimetres. On the other hand, it is undesirable to avoid topics simply because numerical measurement is impossible.

For example, researchers may reasonably argue about whether or not the English Revolution arose out of religious, not political, dissatisfaction, without being able to attach numbers to the extent of each type of dissatisfaction. Similarly, one may reasonably argue that primitive religion tends to reproduce the dominant images a society has of itself, without having to quantify the key variables (in this case, religious imagery and social self-imagery).

The advantage of quantification is that it permits more precise discussion and testing of hypotheses than does verbal description. But precision of this kind may sometimes sacrifice accuracy in the completeness of the portrayal it allows. We lose a great deal of understanding if we reduce the concept of "social class" to, say, income equality; the concept of "ability," to IQ; or the concept of "industrialization," to Gross National Product per capita, or per cent of the work force outside agriculture. Qualitative and quantitative data should be used where they are most appropriate to the meanings of the hypothesis to be tested.

Researchers conceive of four levels of measurement: nominal, ordinal, interval, and ratio:

Nominal level. These measures consist only of named categories: "Anglophone/Francophone/Other," for example; or "male/female." These categories cannot be arrayed on a yardstick running from most to least. They are incomparables, like apples and oranges.

Ordinal. These categories can be arrayed from most to least, since they are all measured in the same units. For example, "big, bigger, biggest" is an array of sizes whose order is known and communicated. We have no doubt that "biggest" has more size units (whatever these may be) than "big." What we don't know is whether the difference in size between "biggest" and "bigger" is the same as the difference between "bigger" and "big." For some purposes, this information may not be important. And in many cases the information simply cannot be obtained. Typically, what we call qualitative research is carried out on variables at the nominal and ordinal levels of measurement.

Interval level. These measures are the ones most commonly used in social-science research. Their categories are an equal distance, or interval, from one another. An example is the IQ test score. The *average* score for a population is 100. It is assumed that the distance between a score of 100 and 110 has the same meaning as the distance between a score of 110 and 120. However, one never hears a researcher claiming that someone with an IQ of 140 is twice as smart as a person with an IQ of 70. The reason is that for IQ scores there is no absolute zero, indicating a complete lack of intelligence. Only such an absolute zero permits the comparison of two levels in the way just mentioned.

To state the same ideas more formally, an interval scale is one in which the rank ordering of people is known with respect to some attribute (e.g., intelligence); it is known how far apart the people are from one another with respect to the attribute; but no information is available about the absolute magnitude of the attribute for any person. Thus an interval scale is an ordinal scale to which we have added information about the distance between ranks. What differentiates the interval scale from the ratio scale is the lack of an absolute zero; this means that in an interval scale, people can only be measured in relation to one another.

Ratio. These scales measure such phenomena as height, weight, and income. It *is* meaningful to speak of someone being twice as tall or rich as someone else, since we can conceive of (and measure) a complete absence of height or money. Attitude measures are often constructed so as to contain a zero score; and in these cases we can claim that one person is twice as satisfied, for example, as someone else (since it is possible to be not satisfied at all).

To hammer home these ideas about different scales, suppose that you are a teacher reading student papers. You may choose to put them into categories, labelling some "creative," others "well organized," others still "full of good information." These categories or labels are *nominal* measures of the students' achievement: they do not rank or grade them in relation to one another.

A true *ordinal* measure would be achieved if you graded the papers from best (first ranking) to worst (last ranking), with no or few ties at any rank. These are ordinally measured in the sense that they are ordered from best to worst, but there is no indication either of how far apart the ranks are, or of what absolute scores correspond to particular performances.

A *ratio* measure would be provided if the teacher assigned to each paper a grade from zero to one hundred. Such grading would provide information not only on rank but also on how close students were to one another in their performance and in relation to the absolute minimum score of zero. (Grading on a pass/fail or letter-grade—"A/B/C/Fail"—basis is a more compressed version of ratio measurement if the corresponding cut-off points are known: for example, that a letter grade of B means 70 to 79 per cent).

An *interval* measure would be provided if you graded each paper in relation to the group average. You might, for example, select the middle-ranking paper and assign it a score of 65 per cent. In a "normal distribution," or what is sometimes called a "bell curve," 66 per cent of cases are one standard deviation away from the mean and 95 per cent of cases within two standard deviations. The teacher might arbitrarily decide to make the standard deviation 10 per cent, so that the 66 per cent of all student papers that surround the middle-ranking paper will receive grades between 55 and 75 per cent; and the 95 per cent of all papers submitted will receive grades of between 45 and 85 per cent, with the remainder receiving grades of 40 to 90 per cent.

In this case, the conditions for interval measurement have been met: students are ranked in relation to one another and the numerical distance between them is specified. But the relation between their grade and a true zero is not known (or is positively obscured). Teachers often grade on a curve in this way precisely because they do not believe that a test or assignment can validly include a score of zero.

Most statistical procedures in common use are designed for ratio, or at least interval-level measures. However, ways of dealing statistically with ordinal- and nominal-level variables are coming into wider use. For further discussion of this topic, we recommend taking a course on research methods.

OPERATIONALIZATION

What it is

"Operationalization" is the part of the research cycle that takes the researcher from concepts to measures. More precisely, it is the specification of procedures or operations that must be carried out to measure a concept named in the hypothesis to be tested.

So, for example, the hypothesis that more-intelligent students will have higher career aspirations than less-intelligent students cannot be proved true or false until we define operationally the key concepts "intelligent" and "career aspirations." If we define "intelligence" as "the score obtained by a student on the Wechsler IQ Test at the age of 14" and "career aspiration" as "the job a student hopes to hold at age 35, as measured by the Blishen occupational-status scale," we can then survey a sample of high-school students, calculate the correlation between measured intelligence and measured career aspiration, and determine whether that correlation is large or small. If large, the hypothesis is considered to have been supported by the data.

Researchers must take care to maintain a distinction between the concept and its measure. They might argue that "intelligence" is more than what an IQ test measures: that it includes creativity and resourcefulness, for example, two qualities that many believe are penalized by the standard IQ test. Likewise, they might argue that career aspiration means more than a student's desired job status at age 35: it may mean an entire pattern of work plans, not a single attainment; or a concern with job satisfaction and autonomy, not merely income and prestige (which the Blishen scale measures).

In this case the quarrel is not about the value of operationalization, but about whether the designated operations faithfully capture the meaning of the concepts the researcher is hypothesizing about. As a researcher you must always take care, in your own work and in evaluating the work of others, to determine whether the planned data-collecting operations are sufficient to address the hypothesis as originally conceived. We shall say more about this when we discuss validity, in the next chapter.

Plan where your data will come from

Once you have determined what your key concepts and intended operations are, you must still specify where and how these operations are to be performed. Things can get out of hand if more than two or three concepts are involved, with several measurements intended for each. You will find it useful to make a table to keep track of what you are doing.

In the first column, note all the key concepts in your hypothesis. Consider the following hypothesis: "The probability of migrating will be proportional to the job opportunities in the place of destination and inversely proportional to the opportunities in the place of origin". The key concepts to be noted are "probability of migrating," "job opportunities," "place of destination," and "place of origin."

In the second column note the corresponding measures or operations to be performed on the data. In respect to "probability of migrating" do we mean "the proportion of all residents who actually migrated in a given year," or do we mean "the stated intention of current residents to migrate in the year ahead," or both, or neither? By " "job opportunities," do we mean "job vacancies" or "expected job vacancies"? In either event, do we mean "all job vacancies," or "job vacancies in the line of work the respondent is accustomed to doing"? And when we speak of "place of destination" and "place of origin" do we mean to compare countries or smaller units—cities or counties, for example? How we answer these questions will determine where we look for our data and how we measure them.

In the third column specify the data source for each operation. If, for example, you are interested in measuring the probability of migration in terms of the observed migration between two countries (e.g., Italy and Canada) during the past year, published or unpublished government statistics will suffice. But if you are interested in measuring people's intended migration in the coming year, in relation to their perception of opportunities in Canada, or more specifically in Toronto, Edmonton, or Moncton, a survey will be needed; government statistics will not fill the bill.

After completing the third column you will know all the data sources that you will have to tap. Then reorganize your information, putting the measures in column two into boxes defined by the data sources noted in column three. By doing this you determine which two, three, or more questions to ask of government statistics; which two, three, or more questions to ask in a survey of current residents; and so on.

If certain data sources (e.g., the plans and attitudes of residents of Italian towns and cities), are not available, certain operations are going to be impossible. You must then decide whether what remains possible — in this case, an analysis of government statistics — will be sufficient to answer the question originally intended to be answered.

Once you have created an information-collecting device — for example, a questionnaire — you will find it useful to go through it labelling all the questions to see how they contribute to the testing of hypotheses. As before, remember that all concepts should be measured by one or more items, and that items with no relevance to your theory should be eliminated.

Define your categories beforehand

Before designing questionnaires or other information-collecting devices, good researchers list the categories of their variables and may even draw up mock tables anticipated in their analyses. These steps direct them to proper measurement — for example, to the proper wording of questions. In the case of complex, multi-dimensional concepts such as social class, job satisfaction, or quality of life, doing so may even suggest additional questions to ask. More will be said about these and related issues in the section on scale construction (p. 88) below.

TWO KINDS OF DATA

We have already noted some of the differences between quantitative and qualitative data: chiefly, that qualitative data may be less precise but in a certain sense more accurate, or "true to life," whereas quantitative data enable us to use the rigorous statistical methods common in the natural and physical sciences.

Some believe that the differences between these two types of data are even more encompassing; that the differences represent paradigms, or ways of viewing data and the world. A comparison of these contrasting paradigms is provided in Figure 4.1.

Figure 4.1
The Qualitative and Quantitative Paradigms Compared

QUALITATIVE PARADIGM	QUANTITATIVE PARADIGM
Advocates the use of qualitative methods.	Advocates the use of quantitative methods.
Naturalistic and uncontrolled observation.	Obstrusive and controlled measurement.
Subjective.	Objective.
Close to the data: the "insider" perspective.	Removed from the data: the "outsider" perspective.
Grounded, discovery-oriented, exploratory, expansionist, descriptive and inductive	Ungrounded, verification-oriented, confirmatory, reductionist, inferential, and hypothetico-deductive.
Process-oriented.	Outcome-oriented.
Valid "real", "rich" and "deep" data.	Reliable: "hard", and replicable data.
Ungeneralizable: single case studies.	Generalizable: multiple case studies.
Holistic.	Particularistic.
Assumes a dynamic reality.	Assumes a stable reality.

Rather than reiterate what is in the figure, we will make a few general observations. First, the distinction between these two paradigms is sharpened here for the sake of comparison. In actual research, social scientists move back and forth between approaches. Even the most rigorous quantitative researchers must depend on insights drawn initially from "softer" sources to develop their theories. All the same, researchers *emphasizing* the qualitative paradigm are "closer to their data" than quantitative researchers. They are more inclined to explore their data and describe what they find; more concerned with how an entire pattern of thinking and acting fits together, with the uniqueness and changeability of the reality they are studying, and with the strange interplay between their own consciousness as observers and the consciousnesses of the people they are studying.

This style of thinking is particularly useful in carrying out case studies, whether the subject be a family, work organization, community, or nation. Qualitative data are most appropriate when the question to be answered is a *how* question: how does, or how did, something come about? How do native peoples assimilate to city life in Canada? How do small organizations accommodate the introduction of computers? How did universal literacy affect the everyday life of English working people? How do homosexuals deal with living in a heterosexual world? None of these questions can be answered without understanding the consciousnesses of the subjects, their subtle social relationships, and the changes and readjustments these people make at each stage of the process under consideration.

Quantitative research, as exemplified by the survey (or experiment), is much better at answering *what* and *why* questions. The first type asks about people's relatively stable properties or relationships: what kind of people vote Progressive Conservative, buy Audis, or marry outside their own religious groups? What are the characteristics of societies that enjoy a high level of political participation, high productivity, or freedom of speech? Such research is hard pressed to explain *how* these characteristics came about, but it can accurately generalize about the probabilities that they will occur.

Quantitative research answers the question *why* (or *when*, or *where*) by specifying sufficient conditions under which these characteristics will occur, not by showing how they actually occurred in a particular time or place. Thus, for example, showing that college-educated women are twice as likely as high-school-educated women to marry outside their own ethnic group does not explain how (or why) the women made the marriage choices they did. Why these women were attracted to their spouses, how they dealt with their own and their family's prejudices—about these issues and countless others we are often left in the dark.

Likewise, experimental social psychology explains why people do things in the sense of showing the conditions under which they might be done. For example, the famous obedience experiments conducted by Stanley Milgram (1975) showed that ordinary people in a laboratory setting would willingly inflict terrible, and in some cases supposedly fatal, electric shocks under the influence of a lab-coated experimenter. This proves that ordinary people are capable of terrible actions under the right circumstances. But it does not prove that the Nazi holocaust, South American torture, or South African apartheid can be usefully viewed as the obedience of normal people in a laboratory-like setting. We ignore the historical context at our peril: for obedience is found everywhere, but torture and genocide are not.

This is not to argue that quantitative research can never enlighten us about the processes of interest to social scientists. Perhaps it would be safest to say that the quantitative and qualitative paradigms, like most other paradigms, are best used as complements to one another, not as opponents. From qualitative research come rich insights and new ideas to be tested by rigorous quantitative methods. From quantitative research come generalizations to be specified and fleshed out by the close study of single cases, especially cases that deviate from the general rule.

Social-science research requires an interplay between these different types of data and data analysis. What follows is a brief discussion of some considerations pertinent to each.

QUANTITATIVE DATA

Content analysis

Data analysis that bridges the gap between qualitative and quantitative data is called content analysis. Its goal is to quantify large amounts of qualitative data for the purpose of generalization.

Imagine that you have read fifty magazine stories about career women. How should you analyse these "data"? You can treat them impressionistically, giving a general impression of what the articles said. Or you can analyse their content by looking for certain systematic patterns and counting their occurrence: for example, depictions of these career women as aggressive or easy-going, attractive or plain, likeable or unlikeable, capable or incompetent.

To do the latter, each story must be "coded" to produce numerical data. So, for example, if the story presents its central character, a career woman, as aggressive, you assign the number value 3 in the category designated "aggressiveness." If the story presents her as passive, you assign the value 1. If no mention is made of her aggressiveness (and you can draw no inference about it from her words or actions), you assign the value 2.

Such data can be analysed statistically, in the same way as any other quantitative data. Their validity is determined by the quality of the coding scheme and the objectivity of the person (coder) reading and interpreting the stories. To establish coder reliability it is extremely important to have two or more people code the same content independently. A high degree of agreement will show that the interpretations are not flawed by the biases of particular readers.

Similar procedures can be followed to code behavioural data for content analysis. For example, Robert Bales (1950) developed a method called Interaction Process Analysis, by which means several observers code the ongoing interactions in a small group observed from behind a one-way mirror. (On the uses of this procedure, see Mills, 1967:30–33.) The recording scheme took note of the affective (emotional) quality of behaviours, the seeking and giving of information, who said what to whom, how, and in what sequence. From such data, generalizations could be made about the rise and practice of leadership in the group, for example. And because the data were coded in such a highly structured way, it was possible to check the agreement between coders: a necessary attribute of any content analysis, whether of behaviours or of documents.

Secondary analysis: reading a table

Much of what the student researcher does will be secondary data analysis: the interpretation of quantitative data that someone else has collected, often for other reasons. You may want to do a secondary analysis because the data you are collecting have never been brought together from separate studies, as you are doing. Or you may wish to verify or reinterpret someone else's conclusions. To do so properly, you will need more knowledge of statistics and data analysis than this book can teach you. But at least you should be able to read the tables in which such data are usually presented and arrange your own data in similar fashion.

The data in a table are arranged according to certain conventions. The dependent variable, the phenomenon to be explained, forms the rows of the tables, while the hypothesized cause forms the columns. Researchers then list the data as percentages down columns and compare percentages across rows to see the effect of the independent on the dependent variable. Table 4.1 presents imaginary data on the differences in mating behaviour between college- and high-school-educated women.

Table 4.1

The Likelihood of Marrying Out, by Level of Educational Attainment

	LEVEL OF EDUCATION ATTAINMENT		
	High School Completed	College Completed	Total
Woman Marries In	160 (80)	120 (60)	280
Woman Marries Out	40 (20)	80 (40)	120
Total	200 (100)	200 (100)	400

* Percentages are in parentheses

The data show that, of 200 high-school-educated women, only 40 (or 20 per cent) married outside their own ethnic group, whereas 80 out of 200 college-educated women (40 per cent)—twice as many—did so. This finding might support the explanation that higher education reduces prejudice, or otherwise promotes attitudes conducive to the mixing of ethnic, religious, and other distinctive social groups.

However, other explanations are plausible. We can test them by adding variables to the table and rearranging the data. These additional variables are called *control variables*. Consider the counter-explanation that education does not so much change people's values as bring people from diverse origins into contact with one another. If this explanation is true, the value of higher education for ethnic assimilation is simply to prolong a person's exposure to people of diverse

Table 4.2

The Likelihood of Marrying Out, by
Level of Educational Attainment and
Where Woman Met Spouse

WHERE WOMAN MET SPOUSE

	At School		Elsewhere	
	LEVEL OF EDUCATION ATTAINMENT			
	High School	College	High School	College
Woman Marries In	25 (50)	75 (50)	135 (90)	45 (90)
Woman Marries Out	25 (50)	75 (50)	15 (10)	5 (10)
Total	50	150	150	50

* Percentages are in parentheses

origins. Let us assume that we have data on where these women met their spouses, whether at school or elsewhere. We add this information and rearrange the data as in Table 4.2.

The data in this table show that when we control for where women met their spouses, the original difference in likelihood of out-marriage disappears. Women who met their spouses in high school are just as likely to marry outside their group as women who met their spouses at college. Conversely, women who met their spouses elsewhere are just as *unlikely* to marry out, whether they received higher education or not. This demonstrates that the second hypothesis (education prolongs exposure to diverse potential mates) is the better explanation, and the first hypothesis (education reduces prejudice) has no support in these data.

Survey design

The survey is the most common type of quantitative research in social science. Its purpose is to generalize about the relationships among variables in a population. That population can be an entire nation or city, or some designated portion of all people: for example, all voters, car buyers, parents, schoolchildren, and so on.

As already noted, survey reasoning begins by showing differences in the likelihood that certain subgroups will behave in certain ways: that college-educated women will marry out proportionally more often than high-school-educated women, for example, or that working people will be more likely to vote NDP than owners of small businesses, or that people will more readily migrate out of areas of high than of low unemployment.

The data are tabulated as in Table 4.1. Then control variables are introduced, as in Table 4.2, for one of two purposes. If the initial bivariate (two-variable) or two-way table shows a relationship between the independent and dependent variable, the purpose of introducing a control variable is to make that relationship diminish or disappear. If repeated attempts to make the relationship disappear fail, we assume that the initial relationship is valid. If introducing a control variable weakens the original relationship, this means that the control variable is intervening in the effect of the independent on the dependent variable, or is prior to both. This fact will force us to refine our theoretical model to include the new variable.

In the example given earlier, our data show that attendance at an educational institution is one of possibly many experiences that will increase exposure to people of other ethnic groups. This doesn't eliminate educational attendance from our model; it merely changes its meaning and forces us to look for other "comparable" experiences that would also increase exposure to "outsider" mates.

There is a second reason for adding control variables, especially where the original table reveals no relationship between the independent and dependent variable. That is to determine what factors, if any, may be suppressing a relationship we had expected to find in the data.

Recall the example (p. 11) of the effect of marriage on suicide-proneness. The relationship proves to be very weak, because marriage is apparently more damaging to women than single status, while the reverse is true for men. Thus in a survey of equal numbers of men and women marriage will have no apparent effect; but if we control for the gender of the respondent the effect will be strongly negative for women and strongly positive for men. Finding third variables that will help to reveal, elaborate, or interpret an initial relationship between two variables is an important part of survey-data analysis. Excellent discussions of this enterprise can be found in Rosenberg (1968) and Zeisel (1968).

Types of Sampling

Surveys are not carried out on entire populations; that would cost too much. Rather, researchers typically sample from the population to get a representative picture of relationships in it. The discipline of statistics has refined sampling procedure to a very high degree, so that—armed with the appropriate knowledge—researchers can know in advance how large an error they are likely to make in generalizing to total populations from relatively small samples.

Sampling statistics tell us how much confidence to have in our findings from a survey sample and, conversely, how many people would have to be sampled to raise the level of confidence to an acceptable degree. Repeated use of samples in political polls, market surveys, and other, purely academic, research has shown that a high degree of credibility can be attached to the findings of a well-conducted sample survey.

Central to conducting a good survey is the drawing of a good sample. Not only must it be large enough to provide the required level of confidence, given the size of the population, but it must be selected by procedures that are unbiased. The least biased surveys are based on random samples, in which respondents are drawn in such a way as to minimize the underrepresentation of certain types of people.

There are serveral types of random sampling. Some are more appropriate (and more practical) in certain types of research than others:

Pure random sampling. The researcher begins with a complete listing of all the people in the population, assigns each person an identification number, and then uses a table of random numbers (or a computerized random-number generator) to select the specific cases to be studied.

Systematic random sampling. In this equally unbiased procedure the researcher randomly selects the first case and then every nth case after that. So, for example, if we were randomly sampling the telephone directory, which we knew contained 500,000 entries, and we wanted to sample 500 cases, we would select the first case randomly, then take every thousandth case after that one.

Stratified random sampling. Here the researcher divides the population into subpopulations of interest, such as male and female, and samples randomly within each subpopulation. This procedure ensures that the resulting sample will contain a pre-designated number of males and females (which cannot be ensured with simple random sampling), yet will be unbiased in other respects.

Cluster sampling. In this approach, which is similar to the above, the researcher divides the population into geographic units and then samples randomly within them. This ensures that the resulting sample will contain as many cases from each unit as are needed, yet will be otherwise unbiased.

Random sampling is not always possible, however. In such cases other sampling techniques are used.

Quota sampling. Consider the problem of drawing an unbiased sample of unemployed workers: there is no list of all workers unemployed at a given moment for the researcher to draw on. Therefore the best strategy is to randomly sample the population and reject all cases that do not meet the study's need: that is, all who are non-workers or who are workers but are not unemployed. This technique is not strictly random, but it is certainly unbiased and can be used, with certain adjustments, to adequately represent the population of unemployed workers.

Availability sampling. This commonly used, inexpensive, but far from random procedure consists in selecting respondents who are easily available to a researcher standing on a street corner or in a shopping mall. The results obtained by this method can only be considered suggestive, not unbiased or representative, since all sorts of potentially important factors will enter into determining who happens to pass by the researcher on a given day.

Snowball sampling. This technique is also non-random, and potentially very biased. A starting sample of respondents provides the researcher with the names of others who might participate in the study. In this way the sample accumulates like a snowball rolling downhill. This technique is widely used where the behaviour under study is particularly rare or covert—for example, drug use or criminal activity—although it is not limited to these cases. Like availability sampling, it provides findings that are suggestive but far from conclusive; it is useful where cost and time, and other reasons for the inaccessibility of cases, would otherwise make the research impossible.

Prepare for non-response bias

Even the most careful sampling may not eliminate bias in the results if certain types of sampled persons refuse to participate. Imagine that we have drawn a random sample of the total population and intend to ask their attitudes towards the current government; but only two-thirds of the middle-class respondents and one-third of working-class respondents are willing to answer our questions. This means that we are twice as likely to get middle-class views as working-class ones, and these views may be widely different. If working-class people are much more critical of the government, our report will badly underestimate the true extent of such criticism.

Several strategies are used to deal with this problem. One is to keep drawing cases randomly until we have the required number of middle- and working-class respondents. Another is to repeatedly approach the people who have not responded, until they have finally and decisively refused to participate. Such follow-ups are often very successful in reducing non-response to acceptable levels. This procedure has the added advantage of avoiding the overrepresentation of too-willing respondents. (Research has shown that people who agree too readily, or even volunteer to participate in studies, differ from those who are more reluctant; such differences may interfere with the results of a particular study, although not necessarily with every study.)

A third strategy is to use weights to compensate for the under-representation of certain kinds of people. In effect, this means counting twice the answers of people who, for reasons of non-response, are only half as well represented as they ought to be. In practice the use of weights can become quite complicated, but it is a widely used and legitimate method. A fourth strategy is to compare the responses of people requiring no, few, or many follow-ups, to see how they differ in attitudes and socio-demographic characteristics. This will provide hints as to the characteristics and views of non-respondents (who can be assumed to be most like those who required many follow-ups).

Where non-response is particularly marked and theoretically important, the researcher may undertake special sub-studies of the hard-to-get population. The final option, of course, and one that is always desirable, is to report biased findings in a complete and open fashion, so that readers can judge the study's limitations for themselves.

QUALITATIVE DATA

Qualitative data are used in all the social sciences, although less often in economics and psychology and more often in anthropology and history;

geography, political science, and sociology fall in between. We have already noted the differences in outlook and purpose associated with qualitative and quantitative data. What follows is a brief, far from exhaustive discussion of some considerations associated with qualitative research.

Document analysis

Document analysis, or documentary research, is especially common in history and political science. It aims to examine and interpret original written records as data about the activities and beliefs of a person or group not otherwise available to the researcher. Such documents may include speeches, books, and essays by eminent persons; parliamentary debates; pamphlets, magazines, and other popular writing; and even legends, folk tales, and objects of art.

The first concern in documentary analysis is to determine the authenticity of the document. Did Mr. x really give this speech at such and such a time and place, or was it someone else, or at some other time and place? Suppose you wish to chronicle the increasing radicalism of some political leader or group through the use of speeches and other written materials. It will make a great deal of difference whether a given speech really was written and delivered by the person to whom it is attributed; and, in this case, whether it came before or after another speech indicating greater or lesser radicalism.

The second concern is the document's "meaning," which may be obscure. Perhaps the document originally appeared in a foreign language, or in old English. Can you afford to risk reading a translation, or must you learn to read it in the original language? Another concern has to do with references to contemporary events, persons, and writings. You cannot fully understand any document unless you are reasonably familiar with the persons, events, and ideas it refers to. Failing immersion in the place and period you are studying, you must read other sources to get the essential background.

But surface familiarity with the words and references in the document is not enough. You also need to understand the nuances, unstated assumptions, and "local meanings" hidden in the document. What is meant if the document refers to an eminent figure — the king, for example — as "dashing" and "gallant" but not "wise" or "good," or to parliament as "overcautious" or "foolhardy," or to a piece of legislation as "radical"? Surely what is "good," "overcautious," "foolhardy," or "radical" in one context may not be considered so in another time and place. Therefore you must first understand the shadings of meaning in the document, and then place these shadings of meaning in relation to contemporary views and debates.

Two main approaches are available for this purpose. One is to examine prevailing interpretations of the document in question: how other researchers have interpreted the document, and their reasons. Every documentary interpretation is the application of a theory about what was going on at another time and place. As a theory it is never the final word on the subject, but it may prove helpful or suggestive to the new researcher.

The other approach is to examine supporting documents: other written materials by the same person or group, originating at the same time and place. The concept of "construct validity" — the tendency of measures of the same underlying phenomenon to point in the same direction (see p. 78) — is no less important in documentary research than in the survey kind. If you understand one document to say that a certain figure was disloyal, sacrilegious, radical, or ambitious, for example, you should support your interpretation with other contemporary materials affirming the same thing, or at least expressing similar concerns.

When you undertake documentary research you are in many respects subject to the same constraints as an anthropologist studying a new culture; a sociologist who has begun observing a juvenile gang; or a political scientist trying to make sense of stated attitudes towards a political party by some group with which he or she has little familiarity. Like them, you must learn the language and unspoken assumptions in which the document is grounded; make and test theoretical interpretations about what you are observing; and test these interpretations for coherence against other information you may have: other documents, other types of information about the society in which the document appeared, and other scholarly interpretations of the same document, group, and society.

Field observation

When you collect qualitative data it is critical to organize them in such a way that you can retrieve them easily for later use. In library research of the kind that historians do, the data are recorded on cards for filing, cross-classification, and reassembly; the chronology of data collection may not be important. In field research by sociologists and anthropologists, however, the chronology of data collection is vitally important in two respects.

First, if the research is concerned with the unfolding of some social process, such as the adjustment of a community to disaster, the assimilation of an immigrant family, or the reorganization of a business enterprise, the timing and stages of the observed process will be as important as the character of the changes.

Second, as an observer you yourself are participating in the observed process, and your understanding of it will change with time. Your field notes will record these changes as well as those in the observed. To keep track of changes in your own understanding, it is important to date all your observations for further reflection.

Field notes, related documents, and collected artifacts (e.g., memos, art, photographs) must thoroughly record the researcher's experiences and observations. Conversations conducted or overheard should be noted in sufficient detail to both capture the meaning of major events and illustrate them for a reader. Behaviours observed and inferences drawn from these behaviours should be noted and interpreted. Do not leave these notes and other materials for interpretation at the end of the project. Rather, examine them recurrently as you look for major concepts, themes, and symbols by which to characterize the complex reality you are observing.

To make sure that you don't become lost in the mass of detail, it's a good idea at several points in the course of your project to recall its central goals: what you were looking for when you went into the field, and what you have found so far. Remember that in the end you will be summarizing your findings in terms of the underlying structures and central relationships in the group or culture you have studied.

As an example of field observation, consider the study of a juvenile court that one author of this book conducted as a doctoral dissertation. The court was part of a larger network of relationships with police, truant officers, probation and parole officers, psychiatrists, and school principals, among others. It had to render hundreds of decisions every year and carry out the treatments (e.g., probationary or psychiatric counselling) deemed appropriate. It also had to contend with a variety of pressures: demands from the community for the control of delinquency, from the child's parents for leniency, from the lawyers for due process, and so on. Yet the written law provided little guidance on how the juveniles should be handled. They could be dismissed, given a suspended sentence, or sent to reform school, among other things, depending on how the judge and others perceived the child, his record of offences to date, and his prospects for reform.

What made the situation even more complex was the fact that professional participants brought conflicting expectations and norms to their decision making. The police, for example, were part of a professional sub-culture with values and behaviours very different from— indeed, opposed to—those of the psychiatrists. Where the police were matter-of-fact and inclined to punish "for the child's own good," the psychiatrists were rather more theoretical, concerned with the child's mental health, and typically more lenient. Where the lawyers were largely concerned with matters of correct procedure and evidence, the probation officers were more concerned with family pathology and the overall well-being of the child, whatever the evidence of his wrongdoing.

This research asked, How does a judge actually make decisions in such a confusing context? And how do the various participants accommodate one anothers' views in order to make possible the ongoing production of justice and treatment year after year?

Answering these questions required observing the court in question for many months; listening for clues of conflict and accommodation; watching the court in session; and talking to the participants to get their perceptions of what would happen and why. It required visiting police stations, riding in police cars to get to know the officers, sifting through informal police records on offences unknown to the court; drinking numerous coffees with probation officers to get a sense of their viewpoint and procedure; and generally becoming a known fixture of the court system. In addition, records of past offenders, other people's analyses of these and other court systems, and scholarly writings on juvenile justice all had to be assimilated.

Once the researcher had a general familiarity with the system, more pointed questions were asked in private interviews. Only then was it possible to ask the right questions and enjoy a reasonable likelihood of obtaining honest answers.

Several key problems must be solved in such a research process. You must get close enough to the situation to understand it, yet stay distant enough to see it objectively. And you must be familiar and friendly enough with the participants to win their trust and cooperation, yet avoid being drawn into their intrigues and conflicts.

How the observer gains entry into such a group is itself problematic. If you arrive as a figure of authority or a representative of some institution, many will be reluctant to express their true feelings and attitudes for fear of punishment. But if you arrive without any group contact or other source of legitimacy, the people you plan to observe will have little incentive to cooperate with you. In this respect, college students are often in the best position to study a group, since they can claim a general interest in learning about group processes without having to commit themselves to any particular point of view or faction.

Once inside the research situation, however, you must still move quickly to connect up with the main factions, the leader or leaders, and with key informants, people who will give you a rapid introduction to the way things work (from their standpoint) and the key players.

It is important to avoid intruding on the way the group normally functions. You must be careful to avoid hints and body language that give away your purposes. You should be quick to listen and slow to talk, present but not necessarily noticed, slow to form and express judgements about the group and its members. Nothing sinks a field project faster than interfering with the group's way of thinking and doing things. At the very least, such intrusiveness will change the situation you have come to study; at the worst, it may result in your expulsion.

Social scientists have long known that their mere presence may influence group functioning. What has come to be called the Hawthorne Effect is the production of changes (especially improvements) in group behaviour by the mere process of observation, which is taken as an indication of interest in the group's well-being. For this reason any researcher (in field situations especially, though not exclusively) should seek to measure the social processes under study as unobtrusively as possible.

Try to use unobtrusive measures

In all research settings, unobtrusive measures — ways of collecting data without the awareness of the person or group being studied — are the best. Because they do not intrude on anyone's consciousness, they are unlikely to influence the functioning of the group (or individual), and therefore unlikely to provoke a reaction, whether positive or negative. Obtrusive measures tend to produce a conscious selection of behaviours and attitudes for presentation to the observer, while unobtrusive measures do not.

In field research you do not want the person observed to know precisely what you are looking for. If, for example, you want to verify in conversations that policemen really are more punitive than psychiatrists, you must introduce the issue casually and at an appropriate time. Forcing the issue — dealing with it too directly, or at a bad time — may lead the people questioned to give you false answers: answers they think you want to hear, or answers that make them seem better or worse than they really are.

The same kind of problem can arise in a survey-interviewing situation. Imagine a study of job satisfaction in which the respondents are manual workers. You ask respondents five or ten different questions about job satisfaction, all of which are evidently on the same topic. Sensing the drift of the questioning, the respondents may decide to answer in a way that is more consistent than their actual feelings, in the belief that they *should* be consistent. The respondents will try in this way to appear intelligent and sensible by exaggerating their own degree of satisfaction or dissatisfaction with the job.

This problem is sometimes reduced by putting the similar questions in different parts of the interview schedule or questionnaire. But respondents are likely to catch on and once again answer consistently. Moreover, they may feel irritated at being tricked, badgered, or otherwise manipulated, and want to stop the interview.

Multiple unobtrusive measures will not have the same effect. They are not evident to the person or group studied. Selecting appropriate unobtrusive measures is often difficult and calls for creativity; and such measures are often unique to a particular problem or group. For example, absenteeism, turnover, and on-the-job drunkenness are probably good, unobtrusive measures of dissatisfaction on an assembly line. They are not as applicable to office jobs, however, and even less so to school situations.

One generally useful unobtrusive measure is the *time budget* — a running record of daily activities that has been used in a variety of research settings to measure activity patterns and, by inference, attitudes to these activities. Suppose, for example, that you want to measure the effects of unemployment on family functioning. You ask all family members to record their daily activities at fifteen-minute intervals over a three-day period. The resulting data show that, in comparison with families enjoying full employment, this family spends little time in group activity (aside from meals). The parent with primary responsibility for earning an income spends increasingly long periods at home, taking on new household duties, while the other parent is now often out looking for a job. The parents spend fewer or less regular hours in each other's company, or with their children, than in comparable families with a regular income. They report that less time is available for leisure activity, suggesting that an air of anxiety and depression prevails. This time-use comparison measures the extent of family disruption caused by unemployment *unobtrusively*: that is, without either intrusive observation of the family or intrusive questioning.

EXERCISE 13

Unobtrusive measures

What factors determine whether a labour union functions in a democratic manner?

1. Define your dependent variable.
2. Suggest behavioural measures of that concept. Do you consider these measures good enough, or will attitudinal measures be needed as well?
3. Consider all the likely factors influencing union democracy. Which can be measured by self-reports of behaviours? Which must be measured by self-reported attitudes?

Pattern matching

Many have held that qualitative research cannot test hypotheses. This view is argued on two grounds: that the measures used are not precise enough to satisfy scientific requirements, and that a single case (most qualitative research is case study) cannot be the basis of generalization, only description and exploration.

Recently, however, more attention has been given to showing how case studies using nominal or ordinal measurement can indeed produce tested hypotheses — hence generalizations — through a process that some have called *pattern matching*. Although pattern matching takes a variety of forms, in general it attempts to assess an overall model of explanation by matching a pattern of predictions to a pattern of observations.

In one type of pattern matching the researcher makes a set of predictions and then matches them against a set of observed outcomes. Suppose our model had predicted that the imposition of bureaucratic rules on a previously unstructured work situation would result in (a) increased tension between the boss and workers, (b) formalization of grievance procedures, (c) intensification of rule enforcement, and (d) withdrawal of informal cooperation and favours between boss and workers. The study of a single case in which bureaucratic rules had been put into force would prove these predictions true or false. The more predictions there are to be matched against observations, and the more often they are proved correct, the more reliable the theoretical model being tested appears.

A second type of pattern matching attempts to disprove the main opposing model(s). If Model 1 predicted results (a), (b), (c), and (d), while Model 2 predicts results (e), (f), (g), and (h), a matching of the observed results with those predicted by each model would indicate fairly strongly which of the two models was the better. The worse Model 2 does in comparison to Model 1, the stronger our confidence will be in Model 1. Sequential elimination of all contenders but one would establish that Model 1 was the best.

A third type of pattern matching uses time-series patterns. As we have seen, changes in the dependent variable should always be preceded by changes in the independent variable if the latter is indeed the cause we believe it to be. Imagine, then, that we can chart changes in the quality of labour-management relations over time. Our model predicts that an intensification of rule making and rule enforcement should produce intensified conflict and the withdrawal of informal cooperation by workers. Though we cannot measure the exact *amount* of each change, we can note when such changes have occurred. If our model is valid, each change in rule making and enforcement will precede an incident of increased conflict or reduced cooperation.

Since timing is extremely important in both qualitative and quantitative research, it is discussed in more detail below.

Sequence (timing)

Time sequence is critical in explanations because a cause must come before its supposed effect. Something that happens *after* a particular effect cannot be considered its cause unless the effect had been anticipated or actively sought, and its anticipation is therefore a cause.

Independent variables operating at the same time as dependent variables are hard to organize into a causal explanation, and call for a systemic design. Independent variables that operate before the dependent variable are easier to handle.

Consider the problem of explaining educational attainment. Suppose that the independent variables in a particular study are social class at birth, intelligence (or IQ), gender, and parental encouragement. All influence the entire process of educational attainment. Some may be more significant earlier, some later, but they are all logically (and temporally) prior to the completion of a university degree. They can, therefore, be causal influences on the completion of a university degree.

Some types of explanatory design deal with time sequence more effectively than others. *Experiments* and *quasi-experiments* are best, since by experimentally manipulating the independent variable, the researcher can ensure that the supposed cause precedes the observed effect. Next most sensitive to time are *longitudinal studies*. These follow a particular group, organization, or society over time, to see which changes occur first, which later. The earlier changes are not necessarily the causes of the later ones, but they may be, whereas the later changes can never be the causes of the earlier ones.

Cross-sectional retrospective studies are less sensitive. They collect data in the present, but ask people to recall things that happened earlier. With such data the researcher attempts to analyse the recalled sequence of events. The reason retrospective studies are less reliable than longitudinal ones is that people tend to forget or distort the past, often dramatically. They have often created their own explanation about why something had happened, and their "theory" may lead them to forget or suppress facts that violate it.

Cross-sectional correlational studies are the least sensitive but most common, because they are the least costly and difficult to carry out. Some of these ignore the time sequence entirely and look only for strong associations between variables, from which causation is assumed. Thus if highly paid workers prove more satisfied with their jobs than poorly paid workers (other things being equal), researchers might infer that higher pay *produces* greater satisfaction; an increase in pay would increase satisfaction: and as an individual worker's pay increased, his or her satisfaction probably increased. However, none of these inferences is really justified by the data.

A slightly more satisfactory version of the cross-sectional design compares units (i.e., people, groups, organizations, or societies) at different "stages." For example, if older workers (or people with more job seniority) are found to be more satisfied than younger ones (or people with less seniority), we might conclude that the process of aging (or increasing seniority) increases job satisfaction. In a similar sense, if industrial societies value education more highly than non-industrial ones, we might infer that, over time, the process of industrialization has changed the value placed on education.

In each instance, the researcher assumes that the unit at a later "stage" was once identical in all important respects to the current "earlier stage" social unit, but changed with the passage of time: with aging, seniority, industrialization, and so on. Such assumptions are rarely warranted but often made. They are at the root of all evolutionary theories of society, most stage theories of human behaviour, and many theories of organizational change.

EXERCISE 14

Measure time sequence

Why do young people drop out of school, and what can be done to prevent it?

Design three explanatory studies to answer this question: a longitudinal study, a cross-sectional retrospective study, and a cross-sectional "stage" study. What are the advantages and disadvantages of each?

REFERENCES

Bales, Robert F.

   1950   "A set of categories for the analysis of small group interaction." *American Sociology Review* 15: 30-33.

Milgram, Stanley

   1975   *Obedience to Authority: An Experimental View.* New York: Harper Colophon Books.

Mills, Theodore M.

   1967   *The Sociology of Small Groups.* Englewood Cliffs, N.J.: Prentice-Hall.

Rosenberg, Morris.

   1968   *The Logic of Survey Analysis.* New York: Basic Books.

Zeisel, Hans

   1968   *Say It With Figures,* 5th edition, revised. New York: Harper and Row.

5
Measurement II: assessing data

To produce trustworthy conclusions, the measures used to obtain data in social science must be both valid and reliable. For this reason it is essential that you know how to assess research findings, whether your own or another researcher's. In the first part of this chapter we will examine the various ways of determining validity and reliability. We will then look at the inevitable problem of flawed data and suggest some ways of dealing with it.

VALIDITY AND RELIABILITY

Measures should have face validity

The way a concept or variable is measured should meet common-sense notions of what the concept means. This is what is meant by the *face validity* of a concept. As an example, consider the concept of job satisfaction as measured by questions asked of workers. These questions should seem plausible to any unbiased and untrained listener. They might include any of the following: "How do you like your job?"; "What things do you like about your job?"; "Would you recommend your job to a friend looking for work?"; "Would you encourage your child to prepare for a job like this one?"; "Would you choose this job again if you were looking for work and knew what you do now?"; "Do you look forward to coming to work in the morning?"; or "Do you feel exhausted and frustrated after leaving the job at night?". All these questions have face validity in that they adequately address the issue of how satisfied a worker is with his or her job, although each does so in a slightly different way.

EXERCISE 15

Face validity

What differences in educational opportunities still exist?

1. What do you understand by "educational opportunity"?
2. How might people differ in what they understand by this term?
3. What data might you collect to answer this question?

Measures should have construct validity

Measures of the same variable or concept should be correlated with one another: that is, they should form scales. A *scale* is a combination of responses to a series of related questions. There are many ways of constructing scales, and we cannot consider them here; the important point is that a scale groups together responses that are believed to measure the same underlying concept. *Construct validity* is the degree to which all the items in a scale are correlated with one another and the scale, as a whole, is distinct from other scales.

Imagine, then, that you had asked all of the questions about job satisfaction mentioned above. You should find that the answers are correlated with one another: that is, a person answering one question positively should be answering the others positively too. Statistical methods exist to measure how strong that correlation between items is, and to help the researcher construct a good overall job-satisfaction score from many related items. (Such a score can then be used with confidence as the dependent, or independent, variable in empirical research).

However, common-sense expectations do not always prove correct. There may be many reasons why certain items do not group together. The most likely is that one or more items have been badly measured. For example, the categories used may have been inappropriate; or the respondent may not have understood what the questions were getting at, and may have thought they were getting at something else entirely.

A second reason is technical. The statistical methods used to construct scales often have very strict requirements about the form of the data, especially the *distribution* of answers. (This issue belongs more properly in a course on statistics.)

A third reason why items may not group together is that the concept being measured is *multidimensional*: in other words, it has many aspects, so that the items group into two or more distinct, uncorrelated scales, each one having construct validity. Such multidimensionality can be seen in people's attitudes towards computers in the workplace. One might expect a series of questions about satisfaction with the effects of computerization to reveal a single satisfaction measure — that is, that people either love computers or hate them — but they do not.

In one study at least, two major dimensions or scales appeared: one measured the worker's approval of the increase in efficiency brought about by computerization; another, the worker's concern about the increase in managerial control that computerization made possible. A worker could be very favourable towards the computer as an instrument of increased efficiency, but very unfavourable towards it as an instrument of increased control. For this reason there may be no single overall measure of satisfaction.

EXERCISE 16

Construct validity

In this country, anti-Semitism seems to be diminishing. How do you account for this?

1. What do you understand by "anti-Semitism"?
2. Suggest a variety of ways to measure anti-Semitism: individual versus institutional, attitudinal versus behavioural, covert versus overt, and so on.
3. What reasons do you have for thinking that these different measures might *not* form a single scale with construct validity?

Measures should be reliable

Measures should be reliable, or fairly stable over time, in the sense that each respondent should answer in roughly the same way six months from now as he or she does today. Marked or frequent changes in response should be explained.

As well, you should ensure a high degree of reliability, or agreement in the responses produced by different interviewers (or coders). These two types of agreement — agreement of the respondent with himself or herself over time, and agreement of one coder with another reacting to the same stimulus — constitute what is meant by reliability in social-science research.

The need for such reliability is obvious. We cannot reasonably explain something in terms of attitudes or behaviours that are constantly changing. Yet people's attitudes *do* change over time. If they change in a random, unpredictable way, with great frequency, a researcher should not use them in an explanation. If they change in predictable ways, however, the explanation should include variables that predict these changes. So, for example, if people's willingness to save or invest money changes with their job security or perception of political and economic stability, we should include measures of these experiences and perceptions in our explanation of saving.

One common way of achieving certainty about your measures is to adopt the ones that other researchers have often used. Widely used measures of intelligence, anxiety, social status, work satisfaction, and family cohesion, for example, abound. They all have known properties: thoroughly considered face validity, statistically tested construct validity, and measured reliability. A scale with high reliability and validity is easily justified in any research, student or professional; one without these features is used at the researcher's peril.

Make sure the variables can vary

In Chapter 3 we noted that constants should never be used in an explanation because they never vary, and explanations require variables. Measured variables should be able to vary as widely as reality does. In general, researchers should ensure that respondents are allowed to give a variety of answers wide enough to capture their true range of feeling. The more widely answers vary, the greater the possibility for a good explanation. And the wider the range of variation that the questions make possible, the more widely the answers will vary. Therefore questions allowing wide variation offer the best chance for a good explanation.

In this respect, variables having only two data points—yes/no; agree/disagree; and so on—are weak. Such relatively unvarying variables should not be used if more finely graded variables can be substituted: yes/no/maybe; strongly agree/agree/no opinion/disagree/strongly disagree; and so on. There is, of course, a point of diminishing returns, where adding more categories adds nothing to the respondent's ability to answer truthfully. For example, asking respondents to judge their job satisfaction on a seventeen-point scale, from immensely satisfied to immensely dissatisfied, will probably not produce better results than a seven-point scale ranging from very satisfied to very dissatisfied. The human ability for gradation is limited, at least in this form.

If very fine gradation is needed, a much better strategy is to use a large number of *yes/no* questions. The answers can then be summed together or otherwise scaled to give a score that ranges widely from very high to very low. For example, if you want to measure how satisfied people are with their lives, you might ask each respondent either to rate his or her satisfaction from 0 to 10, where 10 indicates extreme satisfaction; or to answer ten questions — "Are you satisfied with your work?"; "Are you satisfied with your friendships?"; "Are you satisfied with your home life?"; "Are you satisfied with your sex life?"; "Are you satisfied with your standard of living?"; and so on — where each *yes* answer is worth 1 point and each *no* answer is worth zero. The latter approach, which is preferable, will produce a total score ranging from 0 for some respondents to 10 for others.

If an independent variable doesn't vary much, it cannot "explain much variance" in the dependent variable: that is, it will not appear, statistically, to have a very strong causal effect. If the dependent variable doesn't vary much, the explanatory model as a whole cannot "explain much variance": that is, it will appear that the independent variables, taken singly or altogether, fail to provide an adequate explanation. Failures of these kinds account for many of the non-findings in social science.

There are two solutions to this problem, depending on where the problem originates. If it lies with faulty measurement, the researcher should make sure that revised measures adequately reflect the range of variety in the real world, by sufficiently refining his or her categories to tap the available variance.

However, if the problem lies with the real scarcity of extreme or unusual cases in the world (e.g., morons and geniuses versus people with ordinary intelligence; or saints and villains versus people with ordinary morality), this should be dealt with at the design or sampling stage. One method is to "oversample" unusual cases — that is, select a greater number of extreme cases for study than would normally turn up in a random sample. Such oversampling is justified if the purpose of the research is to explain why people take the positions they do within this range of possible variation.

To take an example, suppose we are interested in studying the reasons why people hold the views they do on abortion. A random sample might show that 10 per cent of the Canadian population is opposed to abortion under any circumstances and 10 percent is in favour of abortion on demand (under every circumstance), while the remaining 80 per cent of the population is sympathetic to both views and somewhat undecided, or supportive of abortion under only certain specific circumstances.

With so many people holding down the middle position, there is little variance in our dependent variable (attitude towards abortion). As a consequence, no matter how many good independent variables we measure—in other words, no matter how many questions we ask, or how refined our categories are—we will still find a weak statistical correlation between the dependent and independent variables: that is, an apparently weak model of explanation.

If, on the other hand, we compose our sample to include one-third opposing abortion under all circumstances, one-third favouring abortion under all circumstances, and one-third in the middle, we increase the range of measured variation in the dependent variable. Doing this shows our explanation—the entire collection of independent variables—to work very much better than it did before.

Pretest your own measures

Respondents may not always understand what a researcher is getting at. That is why researchers pretest their questions on a small sample before using them in a larger study. Such pretesting often includes asking the respondents why they answered what they did in cases where their answers didn't "make sense." Some researchers give the respondents a chance to comment on the survey as a whole, and to offer any additional information they may consider relevant.

In large surveys where, because of the cost, the consequences of mistakes are greater, researchers often pretest questions many times on different groups. This practice has the value of showing whether questions are worded well and of disclosing differences among groups that may be worth further study.

This strategy was used in the classic study of the authoritarian personality by Adorno et al. (1969). Researchers in that study not only pretested their questions and scales on dozens of different groups in various versions, but also checked the responses against other kinds of data obtained by interviewing and projective testing. Only items that repeatedly satisfied the criteria of both face and construct validity across many groups and types of data were used in the final measures of authoritarianism.

Use a native expert or key informant

Cross-national studies are more common in some social sciences than others. Comparing nations is inevitable if the unit of analysis is society as a whole, or some institutional feature of society, such as an economy, a polity, or a work force. Comparing societies is also inevitable if the goal is to show that a certain theory holds universally.

Such comparisons are also useful for cross-sectional correlational studies testing "stage theories," as discussed on p. 75. The effect of literacy on voting behaviour, for example, can be tested within a single society; but since complete illiterates are few — indeed, deviant — in our own society, researchers do better to compare the effects of literacy on voting in societies with quite different literacy and voting patterns. This will typically mean comparing modern with modernizing or pre-modern societies.

The problem in cross-national studies is to develop comparable measures of the key concepts. Standards of literacy may be higher in one society than another. Similar problems of measurement attend most social concepts, including urbanization, poverty, satisfaction, freedom, and inequality. One cannot simply impose the same definition on many different societies. The "social meaning" of a phenomenon (e.g., what it means to earn $10,000 a year, to be poor, or to be aged 16) may vary a lot from one society to another; and people's behaviour is largely influenced by the social meaning — not the investigator's meaning — of that variable. A way around this problem is to use indigenous (local) definitions of concepts.

But suppose that poverty for a family of four is defined in India as income less than $500 and in Canada as income less than $15,000. These different measures give an identical "social meaning," but they violate our common sense. There are, after all, certain material differences in lifestyle associated with these different absolute levels of poverty — differences in nutrition and life expectancy, for example.

There is no easy way to solve this problem of the "two realities," cultural and material. As a researcher, you must at least be aware of the forms the problem takes. Doing so means familiarizing yourself with the societies and cultures you are studying. The best way to do this, if possible, is through discussion with an indigenous expert or key informant.

Such an informant can tell you the ways your key variables are perceived in the foreign country; whether your theory is likely to hold there; and whether the measures you plan to use on data from the foreign country will likely have your intended meaning and produce your intended result.

EXERCISE 17

Local perspective

Is urban life more stressful than rural life?

1. Define the key concepts.
2. Which kinds of communities would you place in the "urban" category, which in the "rural" category?
3. Why might residents of at least some of your "rural" communities consider their community "urban"?
4. Why is this difference in views (i.e., yours versus theirs) important, and how will you resolve it?

LIVING WITH FLAWED DATA

Prepare for flawed measures

Most social-science measures are flawed in some respect. However careful researchers may have been, their measures will still be imperfect in important ways.

First, measures may suffer from respondent reactivity. That is, respondents may react to what they think the researcher is looking for and say things that are not quite true: answers that are more strongly positive or negative than their true feelings. There are many reasons for such reactivity, some more likely in certain situations than in others. The problem is greatest in research on intimate or deviant behaviour (e.g., drug use or premarital sex), behaviour or attitudes about which a controversy is currently raging (e.g., capital punishment, inflation, or abortion), or attitudes towards a group that exercises control over the respondents' lives (e.g., management in a work situation, the police, or government).

Some groups react particularly strongly. For example, immigrants from countries where power is exercised in an authoritarian manner often hesitate to answer survey questions about the police or government, despite assurances that their answers will be treated confidentially. (Of course, in some instances researchers are pleasantly surprised to find that respondents enjoy the opportunity to air their grievances. But we can never rely on this reaction.)

Bias on the part of the researcher and, more generally, biases built into the data-collection process, will produce flawed results. This problem includes questions not asked, or asked in pointed ways that discourage certain kinds of answers (for example, "Don't you believe the government ought to limit the immigration of black people?"). But such biases also include certain types of underenumeration: that is, the systematic failure to count, observe, or survey certain kinds of people or behaviours.

Underenumeration is common in even the best surveys. The national censuses of modern countries always underenumerate by a substantial proportion—perhaps 5 to 10 per cent of the total population in North American censuses. People most likely to be missed are the poor, the transient, and the young. Most surveys are likely either to miss these same kinds of people or to find non-random—therefore potentially biased—pockets of them. Telephone surveys will miss people who do not have their own telephones: again, the poor, the transient, and the young. Door-to-door surveys will tend to select in favour of people who are at home a lot—homemakers, the ill, the unemployed, or the retired—and miss those who are at work, have no fixed address, or are hiding from the authorities (e.g., illegal immigrants).

Studies relying on volunteer respondents are also biased, in that volunteers are known to differ in their characteristics and attitudes, at least towards surveys and experiments, from other more randomly selected respondents. Other kinds of biases infect institutionally collected data: for example, police and court statistics on arrests and convictions. These data are well known to overrepresent the poor, the young, and the transient, and to underenumerate offences by the well-off, the middle-aged, and the socially and economically stable. This is because the expectations of rule enforcers, such as the police, help to determine who will be left alone and who will be processed by the institutions. As well, many crimes go unreported, and charges are often dropped when the offender is well-off or "respectable."

Another statistic produced by government that is often widely doubted and debated is the "unemployment rate." Government critics will often argue that this statistic fails to take into consideration people who would be counted as unemployed had they not temporarily dropped out of the work force (into school or household duties) or accepted part-time or inappropriate work (the so-called "underemployed").

Questions asked of the people processed by institutions will also reflect institutional theories about what causes a particular behaviour (e.g., criminality, delinquency, or drunkenness). This bias has the effect of neglecting variables that may be needed to test a theory.

When social scientists are unable to experiment with ordinary people in natural settings, their ability to devise ideal measures, to control the data collection, and to select a representative sample of respondents will be hampered. They are often stuck with analysing measures that other people have devised, collecting data under unsatisfactory or incomparable conditions, and treating unrepresentative respondents as though they were representative.

Know the social processes generating your data.

The fact that data can be biased by the ways they are collected makes it essential for the researcher to know how data collection affected the data: what respondents were expecting in a survey, how interviewers were behaving, and how institutions carried out their data collection.

You may be able to correct biases you know about. For example, if you know that a particular sampling procedure is likely to capture relatively few poor, transient, or young people, you can get a fair measure of some attitude for all members of society by giving extra weight to the underenumerated social types.

In most cases, however, biases in the data cannot be corrected after the fact. The best cure is prevention.

EXERCISE 18

Institutionally collected data

How do the lives of people living below the "poverty line" differ from those of people above it?

1. Define the key concept in this question.
2. How has it been measured, by whom, and why in that way?
3. Try to find out the validity and reliability of that measure.
4. Can you think of better ways to compare the life chances of rich and poor people?

Combine qualitative and quantitative measures

Understanding why people do or think what they do is very difficult. Qualitative data allow us to understand best, since they invite the respondent to speak, answer, or behave in less constrained ways. By contrast, quantitative measures force respondents to answer in certain fixed categories that may not accurately reflect how they feel.

Because of their limited options, quantifiable answers are easy to analyse with powerful statistical techniques. In this limited sense, quantitative data, because they are more precise, are better measured than qualitative data. But what is gained in precision may be lost in accuracy—that is, in the "true-to-lifeness" of the findings. To solve this problem, researchers try where possible to combine both qualitative and quantitative measures of the same thing.

Qualitative measures obtained by field observation, semi-structured interviewing, or analysis of written materials (e.g., documents, letters, or diaries) can be combined with quantitative measures in a variety of ways. For example, in the authoritarian-personality study mentioned on p. 82, quantitative data were used to make up scales. On the basis of these scales respondents were sorted into high- and low-authoritarianism categories. Then samples of high- and low-scorers were interviewed in a semi-structured, informal way. The respondents also completed projective Rohrschach and Thematic Apperception Tests, which required them to make up stories about largely neutral stimuli—in the first case, ink-blots; in the second, sparse line-drawings of people.

Then the researchers determined whether, in a general sense, the qualitative data agreed with the quantitative data: whether people scoring high on the quantitative authoritarian scales also appeared highly authoritarian in the qualitative data. The two types of data proved to sort people the same way, and when combined gave an exceptionally rich picture of the personality type under study.

Clearly, research findings are rarely conclusive. But, as Hans Zeisel has written in his classic *Say It With Figures* (1968:199), "confidence is increased if the same finding is obtained independently from different approaches. Corroboration from different phases of an interview is one example; corroboration of survey findings through established census data is another." Therefore he suggests that "whenever possible items should be included in a survey that allow such corroboration." We couldn't agree more.

EXERCISE 19

Combining qualitative and quantitative data

Has there been an "information revolution"?

1. Define the key concept.

2. Suggest three quantitative and three qualitative types
   of data you might use to answer the question.
3. Do you expect the six measures to form a single scale?
   Why or why not?

Develop a summary measure or scale

To test a theory, it is better to use many flawed measures than one
alone—to see if alternative measures, taken separately, show the same
pattern of findings, or to create a summary measure or scale by
combining many flawed measures. This method takes advantage of
the virtues of each measure while minimizing the effects of its
weaknesses.

A variety of "scaling techniques" are available, and you will learn
more about them in research and statistics courses. What is important
here is to note that combining flawed measures in scales usually makes
the final measure of key variables more valid and reliable. This is as
true in the scaling of many quantitative items as in the scaling of
quantitative and qualitative items together.

For example, recall the study of family adjustment to chronic illness
discussed in the last chapter. "Family adjustment" is extremely
complex, and difficult to measure with a single item. The direct
question "How well adjusted is your family?" will simply not produce
a valid or trustworthy response in most cases, since respondents may
not know what the question means, or may react against it and give
false answers. It is better to ask many less-direct questions about the
attitudes and behaviours considered characteristic of a well-adjusted
family.

Respondents should be also be encouraged to speak easily, in
whatever way they like, about the way their family functions; from
this you can infer whether it is "well-adjusted" in the sense you
intended. Finally, you might want to watch the family interact. Observing it will allow you to assess the quality of communication and
emotional interplay.

All three types of data should be used to cross-check one another.
Some families will score highly on "adjustment," others poorly,
whichever method is used. In this particular instance choosing a
single summary measure is difficult, but in principle it is possible.
And such a measure will have taken advantage of many different
data sources, each with its own strengths and weaknesses.

The summary measure you select may be a single measure, the one that best correlates with all the others; or it may be the arithmetic (weighted or unweighted) sum of scores obtained by a family on a variety of measures. Combining interval- and nominal-level measures arithmetically may prove more trouble than it is worth, but it can be accomplished by statistical scaling techniques too complex to go into here.

CLOSING COMMENTS

With a good design, good theory, and good measurement in hand, you are ready to argue the merits of your theory. To a great degree, the argument will make itself. If theory and design have been adequately thought out in advance, data that agree with the theory will persuade the fair-minded reader without any need for rhetoric.

But research results are rarely clear-cut, and inconsistent findings are commonplace. Despite our best efforts, flawed data are the norm, not the exception. To make a persuasive case — to make sense in social science — you must show not only that your explanation is plausible, but that it is better than any other plausible explanation. How to do this is the subject of the next chapter.

REFERENCES

Adorno, T.W., et al.

1969 *The Authoritarian Personality.* New York: W.W. Norton.

6
Argument

Now you have the data to test your theory and argue its merit. An argument puts your theory and data together in a coherent, sensible way that can be communicated effectively to others.

This is not the place to discuss the statistical analysis of data in any depth; such a discussion belongs properly to the study of statistics. However, a few general observations about data analysis may be useful as you prepare to make your argument.

Facts don't speak for themselves

Many people are confused about the relation between "facts" and theories. And, historically, many have commented on it. One of the founders of the scientific method, Francis Bacon (1620:Aphorism xxxvi), stated that "we must lead men to the particulars themselves; and their series and order; while men on their side must force themselves for a while to lay their notions by and begin to familiarize themselves with the facts." From this, one of the founders of sociology, Auguste Comte (1855), concluded that "all good intellects have repeated, since Bacon's time, that there can be no real knowledge but that which is based on observed facts."

Yet the meaning of any fact is not self-evident. The statesman Disraeli is said to have observed, caustically, that "there are three kinds of lies: lies, damned lies, and statistics." By this he meant that even facts can be twisted to suit a desired interpretation. They make sense only within a given paradigm, or way of interpretation. This relativity of facts holds true from the simplest to the most complex problem. Is the glass half-empty or half-full? No facts can answer this question. Facts say only how much is in the glass: the rest is interpretation. Do Canadians accept income equality for men and women doing similar jobs? No simple fact or set of facts can answer this question either. To answer it, we must first enter the realm of personal values and conceptual definitions. A complex process of inference from observed facts to conclusions and theories lies between the observed and the observer.

As John Stuart Mill (1859:Chap. 2) wrote, "Very few facts are able to tell their own story, without comments to bring out their meaning." Facts do not speak for themselves: they always need interpreting. Statistics provide forms and standards for examining data so that the reader can have some confidence in the conclusions drawn.

What statistics show

Bacon established that facts—however difficult their interpretation—are needed if we are to really understand the world. The discipline of statistics has provided science with a body of knowledge and tools to analyse facts.

Statistical methods fall into two main types: descriptive and inferential. *Descriptive statistics* help to summarize data in precise ways. *Inferential statistics* allow us to decide whether findings occurred for the reasons we think—that is, because an explanation is correct—or simply by chance. The testing of "statistical significance" falls into this second category. However, significance tests do not measure the substantive importance of a finding; they only show whether it likely occurred by chance. Thus very small effects and weak relationships may be statistically significant, even if their explanatory value is trivial.

Other kinds of statistical procedures help us to judge the relative importance of explanatory variables. Such procedures (including analysis of variance and regression analysis) are far more valuable for understanding the data than significance tests are. Again, we recommend that you take a course on statistics or consult a "user—friendly" text such as Hays (1963) or Harshbarger (1971).

Explore your data

Some researchers believe that statistical testing is cut and dried: that only one or two tests of observed results need be made before drawing conclusions. Others hold that research findings should be explored in a more relaxed and complete way, to make sure of getting everything out of the data that can contribute to an explanation.

Various techniques for systematically exploring data have been devised. They can never replace creativity and patience on the researcher's part. But the methods devised by statistical researchers are particularly simple — which encourages use — and flexible, which means that they are useful with many types of data, and resist excessive influence by a few extreme cases. They provide a good sense of the main story the data have to tell. Examples of this approach are provided by Tukey (1977) and Erickson and Nosanchuk (1977).

Although we can say little about these methods here, we urge you to learn more about them and to use them as intended: that is, creatively. The best explanation will be the one that most completely unlocks the story hidden in facts that the researcher has gathered.

EXERCISE 20

What facts show

Does Canada need a population policy to control immigration? Regional migration? Child-bearing?

Imagine that you have enough time and money to collect all the facts you want. What facts will answer this question? What else is needed besides facts?

TELLING THE STORY

Make sure the discipline supports you

Whatever your own ideas or findings, the ideas prevailing in your discipline count for a lot. If most "professionals" would agree with your explanation you are on strong ground. To make sure, it's a good idea to do a second review of the literature on your topic, to bolster your position and refine your argument (you did the first review at the beginning of your research, when you were devising an explanatory model).

As an undergraduate you are at a disadvantage here, since you are less familiar with the discipline and its thinking than the professor grading your paper is. So do the best you can, while recognizing that you may have missed something. Your instructor will not expect the impossible. But you invite disaster if you ignore the discipline's thinking entirely. More likely than not, what you have thought and studied has been written about by many others. Make a good attempt to learn what they have said and incorporate their thinking into your own. Your argument will be better if you do. It will also be more persuasive, since the reader will know there is a body of thinking behind it, and not simply your own.

At least two sides to every story

In Chapter 3 we noted that in every social science you will find at least two paradigms, or ways of thinking about the world. This means that, to explain your data, you need to take more than one interpretation into account.

Even within a single paradigm more than one interpretation is possible. This is largely because data in social-science research are typically flawed. To be persuasive, therefore, you must either argue both *in favour* of the interpretation you prefer and *against* the best alternative explanations; or attempt to assimilate both into a single explanation.

For example, Canada's observed "conservatism" — its lack of a revolutionary past, and Canadians' greater deference to tradition and authority — can be explained in several ways. One is cultural: Canada preserved a way of thinking, promoted by eighteenth-century loyalist settlers and early British immigrants, that was anti-revolutionary and anti-republican (since it was anti-American). An alternative explanation is economic: Canada, always an economic dependency, first of Britain and then of the United States, has a ruling class that has always encouraged subservience. Ordinary Canadians have been taught or forced to accept a subordinate status within their own country and in the world as a whole. This produces the illusion of conservatism.

Any study of Canadian political behaviour — whether a historical study of government institutions or a contemporary study of voting — will need to examine these alternative interpretations. Each points to a different explanation of the phenomenon under study and, equally important, to different predictions about the future. Each would see different possibilities for change and different ways of bringing change about.

Some scholars prefer to argue in such a way as to sharpen the distinctions between alternative interpretations as much as possible. This approach has the great merit of clarifying one line of theoretical argument through contrast with another. Other scholars prefer to blur the differences, taking elements from different approaches as they seem useful. The philosopher Isaiah Berlin (1953:1, 2) calls the latter thinkers "foxes" and the former "hedgehogs," following the Greek poet Archilochus: "The fox knows many things, but the hedgehog knows one big thing." Noting the vast difference between these two kinds of "intellectual and artistic personality," Berlin describes as hedgehogs those who "relate everything to a single central vision." The foxes, on the other hand, are those "who pursue many ends, often unrelated and even contradictory . . . moving on many levels, seizing upon the essence of a vast variety of experiences [without] seeking to fit them into . . . any one unchanging, all-embracing . . . unitary inner vision."

As Berlin shows, both camps have historically included great, innovative thinkers. So both approaches are useful and defensible, subject to two warnings. First, write for your reader: if the professor reading your paper is — or wants you to be — a hedgehog rather than a fox (or vice versa), do what is desired, whatever your personal inclination. Second, if you are convinced that fox-work — that is, using a variety of paradigms and approaches — is the best way to go, be sure to demonstrate to the reader both that you are capable of understanding the distinctions you are blurring, and that the purpose of this blurring is to better understand or explain your subject matter. In other words, don't let the reader think that you are a fox because you aren't clever enough to be a hedgehog.

A good argument will compare at least two interpretations of the same facts: yours and the best alternatives you can think of. You must be assertive even if the results you obtain do not fit easily within a dominant paradigm, for this may signal an important discovery. Failing to argue forcibly for disconfirmatory findings hurts the discipline by weakening its tendency to renew itself with difficult new ideas.

Good alternatives are usually complementary

No theory is ever certainly right or wrong: it is only better or worse than alternative theories. In fact, most good arguments will prove to be complementary — they will fit together — if their authors are dealing with reality, not simply trying to score points against other theorists.

Researchers have two related goals in making an argument. The first is to test a theory and show it to be better than another one. The second is to understand thoroughly the phenomenon under study. Understanding may mean assimilating the best parts of an alternative theory — recognizing, in the last example, that *both* cultural and economic forces help to shape political behaviour. After explaining the subject of your study, try to create a better theory than you started with: a theory that persuasively combines alternative theories or paradigms, if possible.

This is how a discipline improves. Researchers start with a question narrowly defined within a given paradigm and try to prove their own hypothesis wrong (or right), and their interpretations better than any others. Observations that their theory cannot accommodate are signs that a new, more comprehensive way of thinking is needed. Existing paradigms are burst open when anomalies become too numerous to ignore and too contradictory to accepted thinking. In time new, more complete paradigms are created; and so scientific understanding progresses.

Come down hard

Do not argue half-heartedly. Remember, you may be right and the rest of the discipline wrong. However, if you are really of two minds about a question, be of two minds assertively. Say clearly why a resolution is not possible. Ambivalence is justified if competing interpretations are equally suitable to your data yet cannot be assimilated in a single explanation. Like disconfirmatory results, ambivalence points to the need for new thinking, for a new, broader paradigm.

DEALING WITH DISAPPOINTMENT

Acknowledge shortcomings

Ignoring weaknesses in your argument — logical flaws, or data that don't support your case — won't make them go away. Therefore you should always assume that your readers will challenge you on any weak point that you fail to address.

In fact, if your readers are awake they will be looking for weak points, and will see your failure to address them as an admission that you *cannot* deal with them. Readers who share your viewpoint may make allowances and simply judge your work as sloppy. Others, however, may dismiss your whole argument as weak, in which case all your work will have been wasted.

EXERCISE 21

Coming down hard

Select one of the following timely topics:

- mandatory retirement at age 65
- equal pay for work of equal value
- free trade with the United States

Make your very best argument for or against the issue in question. Now, destroy your own argument with an opposing argument that is even better.

What have you learned?

Bite the bullet

The data may prove you dead wrong. If so, admit it. Don't try to deny what any reader as qualified in data analysis as you are, or more so, can independently judge to be the truth.

Suppose, for example, that you had studied the effects of industrialization on people's behaviour. You theorized that the more people interact with machinery at work, the more likely they are to adopt modern attitudes in other parts of their lives: towards politics, social relations, family life, and so on. Accordingly, you collected data in Third-World countries from farmers, small artisans living in cities, and factory workers. You predicted that factory workers would appear the most "modern" of all your respondents and measured a great many attitudes and behaviours to test this.

A statistical analysis of the data found that experiences with modern machinery had a statistically significant (i.e., non-random) effect on modernity, but one that was much less important than the effect of education. What *most* appears to modernize people is education, not factory work. You were right in a small way, wrong in bigger one. Admit it!

"Never let a little data spoil a good theory"

Researchers respond to disconfirmatory findings in different ways. You may simply conclude, and admit, that you were wrong. You may refuse to do so. Or you may look for the source of the problem in your measurement. This is reasonable, since flawed measurement is the norm in social science, not the exception. The problem may indeed lie here. But if it doesn't, you're back to biting the bullet or adopting another strategy of data analysis.

You could move into a relational-study design and look at deviant cases. To take the previous example, you might compare the highly modern workers with the less modern ones to find conditions under which modern machinery does and does not modernize attitudes and behaviours. In so doing, you might find that although modern machinery has no modernizing effect within an essentially traditional factory organization, where tribal loyalties and traditional forms of authority prevail, such effects may be *facilitated* by a work organization that rewards expertise, productivity, and excellence, and undermines those old loyalties. In other words, the effect of machinery interacts with — is suppressed or magnified by — the form of work organization. In this case you will have improved on the original theory and largely salvaged the argument that modern machinery modernizes people. (Your finding does *not* prove that only the form of organization has an effect.)

However, suppose that no conditions can be found under which the theory holds true. The most useful and honest thing to do is admit that the theory is wrong. Perhaps the error traces all the way back to fundamental assumptions about human nature or social organization. If so, a lot of research based on the same assumptions needs reinterpreting and may in fact be shown wrong.

In this way, admitting that you were wrong may yield more understanding in the long run than excusing the findings on the grounds of poor measurement or conditional (i.e., limited) correctness.

Admit the strengths of opposing arguments

Deal thoroughly and honestly with opposing points of view. Assume that your reader will challenge you if you don't. Failure to give your opponents their due will seriously weaken the credibility of even your best findings.

It's hard to admit the merits of an opposing argument, let alone think creatively within its framework. Yet this is exactly what you should be learning to do as an undergraduate in social science. Ideally, when your education is complete you will be able to take any problem within your field, ask "What would _____ (Marx, Weber, Durkheim, Malinowski, Freud, B.F. Skinner, Milton Friedman, John Stuart Mill, Arnold Toynbee, Adam Smith, Jean Jacques Rousseau, etc.) have said about this?" and give a reasonably credible answer. In this sense, your education in social science should train you to play a wide variety of intellectual roles. You must learn and acknowledge the strengths and weaknesses of all the important theoretical positions in your discipline.

The point of this kind of education is not to make you into a ventriloquist's dummy, but to arm you with the best thinking of the past. By teaching you the problems you are likely to encounter and the ways of arguing around them, it gives you a valuable tool. And you must use it honestly, for your readers have trained in the same way, and can spot dishonesty at three hundred paces.

Remember the immense study of the authoritarian personality discussed in the last chapter. Researchers framed, then tested, the theory that authoritarian adults grew up experiencing emotional repression. According to this theory, a person becomes a racist because (normal) childhood fears and hostile impulses are denied expression:

not diminished, only repressed. In adulthood the authoritarian takes every opportunity to direct (or project) hostile impulses on to vulnerable racial groups whom he or she fantasizes are subhuman, immoral and deserving of punishment. This is a Freudian theory, requiring that we assume each person has a "subconscious" mind capable of changing childhood rejections and disappointments into adult punitiveness.

A "learning theorist" opposed to Freud, however, would favor a simpler explanation, arguing that racist behaviour was learned and rewarded from childhood on: that authoritarians are bred by other authoritarians, without the intervening processes of repression and projection.

Good researchers will consider the alternatives to their own explanations. To make an effective argument you must examine the data to see whether they permit alternative arguments. In the example above, if the data showed that authoritarian adults are no more likely to have had authoritarian parents than non-authoritarian adults, that evidence would rule out the learning-theory argument.

EXERCISE 22

Two (or more) sides to every question

Some believe that instincts play a very small role in human behaviour.

1. What are the strongest arguments in favour of this position?
2. What are the strongest arguments against this position?
3. Do the arguments on one side rule out the arguments on the other?

THINGS TO REMEMBER

Don't be intimidated by other people's ideas

Admitting that other people's ideas have merit doesn't mean giving up your own ideas. But this is especially difficult if your ideas are unpopular. You must keep your head: make your points carefully and clearly and give the opposition its due. If you hold distinctly unpopular views and can defend them, do so.

There is no shortage of unpopular ideas that may or may not be true. In particular, ideas about inequality generate a lot of angry response — for example, the ideas that black people are less intelligent than white people; that unemployed people show less initiative (are more apathetic) than employed people; or that highly paid people are more hard-working than poorly paid people. Each of these ideas is controversial, not only because each points to some inequality but, more important, because there are people who might try to use these inequalities to justify a broader social inequality: higher pay, higher job status, or greater social acceptability for some people than others.

Yet empirical studies have found support for each of these unpopular ideas. Many equate intelligence with the score on an IQ test, and tested black IQs *are* lower in many studies. Similarly, unemployed people *are* often more apathetic; and highly paid people *are* sometimes more hard-working. The important thing is not to deny such data, but to draw appropriate conclusions from them.

Living with an unpopular idea is like adjusting to a death in the family: first you want to deny that something horrible has happened. Then comes passive resignation to the unbelievable, terrible "truth." Finally, you attempt to assimilate the truth in a constructive way.

If blacks do have lower than average IQs, this may result from poorer education, or cultural biases in the questions IQ tests ask. The appropriate conclusion is not that blacks deserve less pay or respect than whites, but that blacks should be given better education and fairer (less biased) tests.

If unemployed people are more apathetic, this may tell us less about the *causes* of unemployment than about the deadening, disheartening *effects* of unemployment. Far from deserving less help, unemployed people may need more help in feeling worthy, mobilizing politically, and, of course, finding a job.

Finally, if highly paid people are more hard-working, often even "workaholics," this may direct our attention to the reasons why people work hard. If hard work is something we want to stimulate in our society, we may need to pay ordinary workers better, and give them more challenges and satisfaction in their work than they presently enjoy.

By addressing the unpopular idea creatively rather than fleeing from it, you may contribute something socially as well as theoretically valuable. But to get to this stage you must keep your head. Don't be put off by other people's aggressive reactions against what you are saying. They may think they know where you are headed; but you have every right to demand a full hearing.

Deal fairly with the data

Just as you should not be intimidated by other people's ideas and by the aggressive way they are put forward, neither should you argue in an intimidating, obnoxious fashion. Emotional appeals to decency, morality, or common sense count for nothing in a logical argument. In fact, they undermine your credibility; they supply unnecessary rhetoric and excitement instead of calm reason.

Our goal is "value neutrality." This does not mean that we should be indifferent towards alternative topics of research or research outcomes. As human beings and citizens, we should invest ourselves fully — our hearts, as well as our brains — in the things we study and debate. This means choosing to study and argue for things that matter. We cannot easily be unemotional about such things. We may want it to be true that some underprivileged group is more deserving than some privileged group; that some malfunctioning social institution is recognized as bad and forced to change; or that some cruel society is censured. Defending Naziism or apartheid, or justifying police brutality or the starvation of the poor on welfare, do not rate a high place on many people's research agendas.

However, once you have chosen a problem that is personally significant you must deal with it fairly, remaining unbiased and unemotional in your data collection, analysis, and argument. This "value neutrality" is the essence of scientific truthfulness. Valid results established in this way can then be used confidently in the emotional, political world of action.

EXERCISE 23

The price of emotionalism

Write a very emotional one-page analysis of the costs of pollution to society. Then write a one-page unemotional reply by the president of a major industrial polluter. Ask a friend which one is more persuasive.

What have you learned?

Don't rally strange bedfellows

Be fair in reporting the literature. If the literature goes against your argument, say so and deal with the problem honestly. If you haven't read the literature, don't pretend a false knowledge. Whatever you do, don't let disappointment, haste, sloppiness, or an unwillingness to accept your own findings lead you to fake footnotes or make other assertions that can easily be shown to be false. Sad to say, such fakery is not uncommon. If your reader takes the time to check your references and finds them incorrect, your entire work will be thrown into question. So do footnote and cite your sources thoroughly *and* scrupulously.

Another form of fakery is the use of "tainted" authorities to bolster your argument: published works that lack scholarly acceptance, are taken out of context, or misinterpreted to your benefit; published data you know to be untrustworthy or irrelevant; and earlier theories that are so general or vague as to be open to almost any interpretation. Published social-science research is so diffuse that you can find anything there, to support any position.

A few selected authorities supporting your argument are no substitute for good theory and good data. At best, authorities can make your good theory and good data look better. They cannot turn a bad argument into a good one.

A second point to remember is that individual "authorities" have often said a great many things. If they are great thinkers, their thinking will have evolved over time, modifying and even rejecting earlier ideas. How to deal with the early ideas — what status to give them in the field — is a problem to consider.

For example, Marx's early unpublished manuscripts were much more concerned than later writings with the psychological aspects of alienation. However, the legitimacy of his later work cannot be used to legitimize the earlier work, especially if we cannot show a clear connection between the two. Marx, after all, made no explicit attempt to connect his early manuscripts with his later conclusions in the masterwork *Capital*.

A third point is that authorities should not be used indiscriminately. Using Marx to support one part of your argument, Freud to support another, and Adam Smith to support a third is no argument: it is an intellectual fruit salad. Your three selected authorities in this case are so different, their concerns, assumptions, and conclusions so at variance with one another, that unless you are exceptionally brilliant you cannot bring them together in a single argument. It's better not to try. This is a good reason for working within a familiar paradigm, rather than across several. That way at least you can try to do justice to one way of thinking.

Although instructors vary in this regard, it is often permissible to defend your argument with references to scholars from "outside" disciplines—to cite sociologists in an anthropology paper, for instance, or economists in a sociology paper. But the majority of your references should be to scholars within the discipline you are writing for. Doing otherwise—filling a sociology paper with references to psychology, or a political-science paper with references to philosophy—is not only unlikely to convince your professor; it may also suggest that you have plagiarized the paper, or that you are submitting the same work for two very different courses.

CLOSING COMMENTS

Try your arguments on the people you studied

Once researchers feel they understand the people they have studied, they sometimes tell them what they have concluded. This procedure helps to refine their argument by confronting additional, unnoticed facts, or facts that don't fit in. It is dangerous because it tests the researcher in the hardest possible way, but if the argument passes *this* test, it has a good chance of passing every other. If at all possible, therefore, you should try to perform it.

Confronting the people studied is more common in applied research than in basic research. And it is not foolproof, since the subjects may not understand themselves as well as the researcher does. Still, one is likely to learn something useful in this way.

Consider, for example, a study of Canada's declining fertility. Annual birth records show that fewer children are being born to Canadian women than in past decades, but that the women bearing them are older. In the past, older women bearing children had already borne many. How do we explain this interesting paradox?

We might begin by analysing already existing survey data on fertility decisions, and with these data develop and test a theory about the timing and numbers of children that women are bearing. But to find out whether this theory is valid, the researcher would do well to conduct intensive interviews with selected samples of women: for example, with women who have followed the typical pattern (few children, borne in their thirties) and other women who have violated the pattern (women who have borne many children early in life, or no children at all.) These interviews may not be numerous enough to persuade statistically, but they are useful in checking the theory, illustrating the late versus early child-bearing decisions with quotes and anecdotes, and most important, getting a reaction to the researcher's theory. Such a procedure, less common than it should be, has the dual advantage of confronting a theory with the people theorized about and of corroborating a finding with various types of data, as Zeisel suggested (above, p. 87).

Try the "laugh test"

Tell your explanation to a disinterested person—your mother, perhaps, or a classmate. If doing so makes you feel ridiculous or, worse, provokes laughter, your argument may be deficient. You should think again.

The "laugh test" is not a sure thing. It may simply prove that you or your listener are insecure, or think that explaining things is a ridiculous, laughable enterprise. If so, take a deep breath; try to remember the purpose of social science; find another listener; then do it again.

Even better, use the laughter to your advantage. Have fun. Think of what you are doing as a game whose object is to persuade—and the process of persuasion can be fun. If you find yourself working too hard, you are probably not winning the game. Strive for elegant simplicity, bold reasoning, and clean data: this is the social scientist's motto.

If excessive laughter persists, take two aspirins and an astronomy course.

EXERCISE 25

The laugh test

What purposes are served by sending criminals to prison?

Now consider the following answers. Which of these pass the "laugh test"?

We send criminals to prison . . .

(a) to reform their character.
(b) to teach them job skills.
(c) to prepare them for life outside prison.
(d) to help them make good social contacts.
(e) to build their self-esteem.

Can you invent an answer that passes the laugh test?

REFERENCES

Bacon, Francis

  1620   *Novum Organum*.

Comte, Auguste

  1855   *The Positive Philosophy*. Translated and condensed by Harriet Martineau. 3 vols. New York: Calvin Blanchard.

Erickson, B.H., and T.A. Nosanchuk

  1977   *Understanding Data*. Toronto: McGraw-Hill Ryerson.

Harshbarger, Theodore

  1971   *Introductory Statistics: A Decision Map*. New York: Macmillan.

Hays, William L.

  1963   *Statistics for Psychologists*. New York: Holt, Rinehart and Winston.

Mill, John Stuart

  1859   *On Liberty*.

Tukey, John W.

  1978   *Exploratory Data Analysis*. New York: Addison-Wesley.

7
Writing a research report

Research reports in the social sciences follow certain conventional patterns. Differing in many respects from essays and book reports, they are rather more similar to scientific or technical writing in the "hard sciences." Typically, the report follows a sequence of presentation that mirrors the stages of the research project itself as we have outlined them in this book: design, theory, measurement, and argument. We will discuss each of these in turn as they relate to the writing of a research report.

OBJECTIVES (DESIGN)

The first section of a research report is typically called *Objectives*, *Goals*, or *The Research Problem*. It corresponds to what we have called *design* in that it provides a general overview of the structure of the research task. This section states the topic to be discussed or question to be answered. It also indicates whether the goal of the report is a relatively unstructured description and exploration or one of the more highly structured approaches we have discussed at length: explanation, prediction, an examination of conditional relationships or the study of a system of relationships.

Many reports indicate the anticipated practical or theoretical value of the research. Where the research is justified on the grounds of its social utility, the author may want to provide some facts about the magnitude of the problem to be solved and the ways in which the research may help to solve it. Where the value of the research lies in its contribution to a scholarly debate, the author is led directly into the next section of the paper, the "literature review," which is a close discussion of these debates.

So, for example, you might begin a research paper on teenage suicide by stating that its purpose is to gather and analyse comparative cross-national data on recent trends. You could note that in many countries teenage suicide is rapidly becoming a major cause of death among young people; that the rise in teenage suicide rates is considerably higher in certain countries than in others; and that the purpose of the paper is to understand the reason for this difference in trends. You might then suggest some practical benefits that may flow from such knowledge—for example, steps that governments or schools might take to reduce the tendency to suicide in countries with the fastest growing rates; or theoretical benefits that may follow—such as a better understanding of the ways certain social or cultural arrangements (e.g., excessive competitiveness in school performance) may contribute to the creation of the problem.

BACKGROUND (THEORY)

The next section of the paper, typically called *Background*, *Previous Research*, or *Literature Review*, reflects the *theory* behind research. Its purpose is to review briefly, systematically, and thoroughly the current state of knowledge about the problem under consideration.

To write this section of the report you must first review the literature. In many areas the existing literature is extremely voluminous, running to dozens or even hundreds of books and articles. Worse, these books and articles may be spread through a variety of journals and library locations. For example, you could look for literature on teenage suicide in journals and books in the fields of sociology, psychiatry, psychology, social work, family studies, epidemiology, and family medicine, to name only a few. It is certainly not possible to carry out a credible literature review by the hit-and-miss method of rummaging through a few textbooks in a single field of social science.

The best solution to this problem, and one that is increasingly common, is a computerized literature search. You ask your university librarian to search all of the computerized data bases that may be relevant: in this case, sociology, psychiatry, psychology, and so on. The computer is instructed to print the titles, references, and (if desired) abstracts of all books and articles with *teenage* and *suicide* in their titles or abstracts. To search effectively, the computer must also look under equivalent keywords (for example, substituting *adolescent* for *teenage*). The result may be a great many references produced within hours rather than weeks.

The computerized literature search is not yet widely used by undergraduate students. Some libraries do not provide such a service, although their number is shrinking rapidly. Further, many students may not know that the service is available, or may consider it prohibitively expensive. In fact, it is relatively inexpensive compared with the dozens or hundreds of hours that you would need to produce an equally good review. However, it does cost something: the cost is proportional to the number of different data bases that the computer must search, and the number of entries located in a given data base. Before you decide against a computer search, at least get a cost estimate from the librarian.

A second very satisfactory approach is to search out bibliographies on the topic in question. A good library will contain many bibliographies and review articles either in print or in typescript. They may apply directly to the problem you are investigating, or they may point to other sources that are more directly applicable. The problem with bibliographies and review articles is that they are quickly outdated by advances in knowledge, while a computerized data base is constantly updated. Once located, however, bibliographies and review articles cost nothing to use. Locating them can be made immeasurably easier by a talk with your university reference librarian.

A third approach is to compile your own bibliography. To do this, look through the published abstracts of relevant research in your library. You will, in effect, be doing manually what the computer does, much more quickly, in its literature search: namely, looking for keywords indicating that a completed project has some bearing on the project you are about to begin. Then select one or more textbooks or journals in the research areas most likely to contain references to your problem of interest. These should be as recent as possible. Work backward in time to locate articles with good literature reviews. Note the sources cited on cards; then start to read these sources, the most recent ones first, noting additional sources on cards as you go. After a certain point the number of new sources will start to decline, and you will see that certain sources have been mentioned many times. Make sure to read those multiple-mention sources carefully, and read as many of the others as you have time for.

Whichever method you use, you will soon have a collection of research findings on your topic of interest. Your task is then to put these into meaningful order. You should be looking for (a) findings that are repeated so often as to seem unassailable; (b) findings that are sharply contested; and (c) theories that seek to explain these findings.

Your goal here is to use the literature review to sharpen your own thinking about your research problem to the point where you can state hypotheses—predictions that can be tested with the data you will collect (see pp. 26-8).

For example, the literature may show that suicides by teenagers are most common around examination time; that teenage-suicide notes generally reflect a concern with academic and other kinds of personal failure; that suicide is more common among career-conscious middle-class children than job-conscious working-class children; and that boys, being more career-conscious than girls, are also more suicide-prone. These findings would suggest the following hypotheses: (a) teenage suicide will rise in periods when adults are expressing greatest concern about the job market and their children's career prospects, and will decline in periods of economic prosperity; and (b) teenage suicide will be greatest in countries where educational "streaming" is most severe—that is, where a child's life chances will be largely determined by a set of examinations taken in adolescence. Hypothesis (a) predicts that North American suicide rates for teenagers will be higher in the periods 1975-85 and 1929-39 (i.e., periods of high unemployment) than in 1955-65 (i.e., a period of economic growth and high employment); while hypothesis (b) predicts that suicide rates for teenagers will be higher in Japan, France, and England (where educational streaming prevails) than in Canada and the United States (where it does not). Your research goal is now to test these hypotheses.

METHODS (MEASURES)

The next section of the paper, typically called *Methods*, may include subsections called *Indicators* (or *Measures*), *Sampling*, and *Data Collection*. This is the section in which you put your hypotheses to the test.

In the example we have been considering, your goal will be to collect thorough and reliable data on teenage suicide in different times and places. To find them you will have to look in published official statistics. You must also ensure that these statistics are comparable: for example, that they define death by suicide in the same ways and provide statistics in the same age groupings. Where the data are not strictly comparable, they must be adjusted to be as comparable as possible.

This section of the paper is often quite long and complex, especially if you have had to create a special data-collection instrument or procedure for coding published statistical data. Since scientists assume that the quality of research findings is no better than the research methods used to produce them, your readers will want a great deal of information about what you did to get your results. For this reason, the "measures" section of a research paper may be the longest one of all.

RESULTS (ARGUMENT)

The final section of a research paper is typically called *Results* (or *Findings*), with subsections often headed *Data Analysis*, *Conclusions*, and *Discussion*. Taken together, these make up the portion of the report that we have called the "argument." Its purpose is to present and interpret the data collected; to judge whether they supported the hypotheses; and, based on that judgement, to draw conclusions about the theory that gave rise to the hypotheses. The section, and paper, may end with a modified version of the original theory and suggestions for further research that will test the revised theory.

To continue our example of teenage suicide, we may find that our hypotheses are partly valid and partly invalid. The data may show that, although teenage suicide rates were higher during the recession of 1975-85 than during the boom of 1955-65, both rates were higher than during the Depression of 1929-39. Likewise, they may show that although teenage suicide rates are consistently higher in Japan and France than in Canada and the United States, they are no higher in England than in Canada; and further that the difference in rates between Canada and the United States is as great as that between the United States and Japan. These findings, while partly supporting our theory, contain too many anomalies for comfort.

The next task would be to attempt to account for these anomalies. Was the original theory wrong? Or do some other factors, yet unexamined, also enter into the explanation? If the latter, what might these factors be, and how might we conduct a project to determine whether they really are contributing to teenage suicide?

In this way a good research project reaches backwards and forwards: backwards, by situating itself in the existing literature of competing findings and theories; forwards, by contributing new findings, revised theories, and suggestions for further research that will refine our understanding of the topic. While it may be too much to expect that a student research paper will often provide a breakthrough in knowledge, or even a significant reinterpretation of the problem, it is not too much to expect that it will demonstrate a grasp of the purposes, conventions, and techniques of social-science research, however miniaturized.

You will note that in scholarly journals almost every article is preceded by a brief *abstract* providing a capsulized version of the entire report. About one double-spaced page in length, this section is extremely useful for the reader. And although abstracts are not generally required for student work, writing one may also help you to see more clearly what you have accomplished. (In an applied-research project written for government or business, such an abstract is expanded to several pages in length and is called an *Executive Summary*. Since it is often the only part of the report read closely by most readers, it assumes a great deal of importance for the researcher. This is another reason for learning how to miniaturize your own work: it may come in handy later on in your report-writing career).

We should finish this brief discussion by reminding you that it is far better to do a good job on a small problem (or a small portion of a big problem) than to do a poor job on too big a problem. Remember, too, that every research project will get bigger than you had anticipated as you carry it out. So start small and let the project grow. If you do this with a problem worth researching, you cannot fail to produce something of value.

8
Writing
an essay

If you are one of the many students who dread writing an academic essay, you will find that following a few simple steps in planning and organizing will make the task easier—and the result better.

THE PLANNING STAGE

Some students claim they can write essays without any planning at all. On the rare occasions when they succeed, their writing is usually not as spontaneous as it seems: in fact, they have thought or talked a good deal about the subject in advance, and come to the task with some ready-made ideas. More often, trying to write a lengthy essay without planning just leads them to frustration. They get stuck in the middle and don't know how to finish, or suddenly realize that they are rambling off in all directions.

In contrast, most writers say that the planning, or pre-writing, stage is the most important part of the whole process. Certainly the evidence shows that poor planning usually leads to disorganized writing; in the majority of students' essays the single greatest improvement would not be better research or better grammar, but better organization.

This insistence on planning doesn't rule out exploratory writing (see p. 119). Many people find that the act of writing itself is the best way to generate ideas or overcome writer's block; the hard decisions about organization come after they've put something down on the page. Whether you organize before or after you begin to write, however, at some point you need to plan.

Reading primary material

Primary material is the direct evidence—usually books or articles—on which you will base your essay. Surprising as it may seem, the best way to begin working with this material is to give it a fast initial skim. Don't just start reading from cover to cover: first look at the table of contents, scan the index, and read the preface or introduction to get a sense of the author's purpose and plan. Getting an overview will allow you to focus your questions for a more purposeful and analytic second reading. Make no mistake: a superficial reading is *not* all you need. You still have to work through the material carefully a second time. But an initial skim followed by a focused second reading will give you a much more thorough understanding than one slow plod ever will.

A warning about secondary sources

Always be sure you have a firm grasp of the primary material before you turn to secondary sources (commentaries on or analyses of the primary source). Some instructors discourage secondary reading in introductory courses because they know the dangers of relying too heavily on it. If you turn to commentaries as a way around the difficulty of understanding the primary source, you may be overwhelmed by the weight of authority, and your essay will be trite and second-hand. Your interpretation could even be downright wrong, since at this stage you may not know enough about a subject to be able to evaluate the commentary. Secondary sources are an important part of research, but they can never substitute for your own active reading of the primary material.

Analyse your subject: ask questions

Some instructors ask students to choose their own essay topics, and others simply suggest subject areas. In either case, since a subject area is bound to be too broad for an essay topic, you will have to analyse it in order to find a way of limiting it. The best way of analysing is to ask questions that will lead to useful answers.

How do you form that kind of question? Journalists approach their stories through a five-question formula: *who? what? where? when? why?* You could apply the same formula to aspects of your subject, and add *how?* For example, starting with the question *what?* and applying it to political organization, you might ask "What are the differences between a dictatorship and a democracy?"; "What is the role of the judiciary in each?"; "What are the best qualities and worst flaws of successful leaders under each type of system?". *How* and *why* questions are often the most productive, since they take you beyond information-gathering and force you to analyse and interpret. If you are considering the Canadian constitution, for example, you might ask "How are the courts likely to be affected by the new constitution?"; "Why was education left to the provinces?"

Try the three-C approach

A more systematic scheme for analysing a subject is the three-C approach. It asks three basic questions about *components*, *change*, and *context*:

What are the components of the subject? In other words, how might it be broken down into smaller elements? This question forces you to take a close look at the subject and helps you avoid over-simplification. Suppose that your assignment is to discuss the policies of Mackenzie King. After asking yourself about components, you might decide that you can split the subject into (1) domestic policies and (2) foreign policies. Alternatively, you might divide it into (1) economic policies, (2) social policies, and (3) political policies. Then, since these components themselves are fairly broad, you might break them down further. Economic policies might be split into fiscal and monetary policies; political policies could be split into relations with the provinces and relations with other countries.

What features of the subject reflect change? For example, did Mackenzie King's policies in a certain area alter over a period of years? Did he express contradictory views in different documents? What caused changes in policy? What were the effects of these changes?

What is the context of this subject? Into what particular school of thought or tradition does it fit? What are the similarities and differences between this subject and related ones? For example, how do Mackenzie King's policies compare with those of other Liberal Prime Ministers? With Conservative policies?

General as most of these questions are, you will find that they stimulate more specific questions—and thoughts—about the material, from which you can choose your topic and formulate a thesis. Remember that the ability to ask intelligent questions is one of the most important, though often underrated, skills that you can develop for any work, in university and outside.

Analysing a prescribed topic

Even if the topic of your essay is supplied by your instructor, you still need to analyse it carefully. Try underlining key words to make sure that you don't neglect anything. Distinguish the main focus from subordinate concerns. A common error in dealing with prescribed topics is to emphasize one portion while giving short shrift to another. Give each part its proper due—and make sure that you actually do what the instructions tell you to do. To *discuss* is not the same as to *evaluate* or *trace*; to *compare* means to show differences as well as similarities. These verbs tell you how to approach the topic; don't confuse them.

Develop a hypothesis

As we have seen in Chapter 3, the hypothesis plays an essential role in the research cycle. But a hypothesis can also be useful in a more general way, even when the essay you are writing does not require a specific thesis. In fact, most students find it helpful to think of any academic essay as a way of demonstrating or proving a point, since the argumentative form is the easiest to organize and the most likely to produce forceful writing. In such cases your hypothesis need be nothing more than a working thesis—an intended line of argument, which you are free to change at any stage in your planning. It works as a linchpin, holding together your information and ideas as you organize. It will help you to define your intentions, make your research more selective, and focus your essay.

At some point in the writing process you will probably want to make your hypothesis into an explicit thesis statement that can appear in your introduction. Even if you do not, however, you should take the time to develop your working thesis carefully. Use a complete sentence to express it, and above all make sure that it is *limited*, *unified*, and *exact* (McCrimmon, 1976:18).

Make it limited

A limited thesis is one that is narrow enough to be workable. Suppose, for example, that your general subject is the Social Credit party in Canada. Such a subject is much too broad to be handled properly in an essay of one or two thousand words: you must limit it in some way and create a line of argument for which you can supply adequate supporting evidence. Following the analytic questioning process, you might find that you want to restrict it by time: "The Social Credit party in the 1970s was indistinguishable in its monetary policies from the Conservative party." Or you might prefer to limit it by geography: "The development of the Social Credit party in British Columbia had less to do with its policies than with its political opportunities." To take an example from anthropology, suppose that your general subject for a two-thousand-word essay is the role of religion. You might want to limit it by discussing a prominent religious ritual in one or two societies. So, for example, you might discuss how ritual dancing in one society directly expresses a prayer for divine intervention in a hunt or battle, whereas in another society dancing has no obvious goal but to promote a sense of ecstasy and social communion. Whatever the discipline or subject, make sure that your topic is restricted enough that you can explore it in depth.

Make it unified

To be unified, your thesis must have one controlling idea. Beware of the double-headed thesis: "In his term as President of the United States, Lyndon Johnson introduced many social programs, but the Vietnam War issue led to his downfall." What is the controlling idea here? The success of Johnson's social programs, or the reason for his downfall? The essay should focus on one or the other. It is possible to have two or more related ideas in a thesis, but only if one of them is clearly in control, with all the other ideas subordinated to it: "Despite criticism from various regions in Canada, the CBC is an instrument of national unity."

Make it exact

It's important, especially in a thesis, to avoid vague terms such as *interesting* and *significant*, as in "Helmut Schmidt was Germany's most interesting Chancellor." Does *interesting* mean *effective* or *daring* in his policies, or does it mean personally *charming*? Don't simply say that "Freud's analysis of dreams is an important feature of his writing" when you can be more precise about the work you are discussing, the kind of dreams he analysed, and what he inferred from them: "In his study of the 'Wolf Man' Freud uncovered important clues about the ways people repress and reinterpret childhood experiences, which come to light in dreams and bizarre behaviour." Remember to be as specific as possible in creating a thesis, in order to focus your essay. Don't just make an assertion—give the main reasons for it. Instead of saying simply "Many westerners are resentful of central Canada" and leaving it at that, add an explanation: " . . . because of historic grievances, such as tariffs and freight rates, and contemporary issues such as the energy policy and the new constitution." If these details make your thesis stylistically cumbersome, don't worry. A thesis is only a planning device, something to guide the organization of your ideas. The wording doesn't have to be the same in your final essay.

Research your topic

If your topic requires more facts or evidence than the primary material provides, or if you want to know other people's opinions on the subject, you will need to visit the library for research. Some students like to read around in the subject area before they decide on an essay topic; for them, the thesis comes after the exploration. You may find this approach useful for some essays, but generally it's better to narrow your scope and plan a tentative thesis before you turn to secondary sources—you'll save time and produce a more original essay.

Explore the library

The importance of getting to know your way around a library can't be stressed enough. You don't want to be so overwhelmed by its size and complexity that you either scrimp on required research or waste time and energy trying to find information. Remember that most academic libraries have orientation seminars specifically designed to show you where and how to find what you want—how to use a card catalogue, for example. Take advantage of these services. Librarians will be glad to show you the bibliographies, indices, and other reference books for your field of study. Once you are familiar with these basic sources you will be able to check systematically for available material. (For more information on library research, see pp. 106-7.)

Taking good notes

Finding your research material is one thing; taking notes that are dependable and easy to use is another. With time you will develop your own best method, but for a start you might try the index-card system. Record each new idea or piece of evidence on a separate card (see p. 11); the number you need will obviously depend on the range and type of your research. When you've finished with your note-taking, you can then easily arrange the cards in the order in which you will use them.

Whatever method you follow, remember that exact records are essential for proper footnotes:

1. For every entry check that the bibliographic details are complete, including the name of the author, title, place and date of publication, and page number, as well as the library call number. Nothing is more frustrating than using a piece of information in an essay only to find that you aren't sure where it came from. If

ARNOLD J. TOYNBEE, A Study of History.
Abridgement of vols. I-IV by D.C. SOMERVELL
(New York and London: Oxford Univ. Press, 1946).

Says 20th century follows "typical pattern of
a time of troubles: a breakdown, a rally and
a second relapse" (p.553).

you take several ideas from one source, it helps to put the main
bibliographic details about the author and work on one card,
and then use a separate card for each particular idea or theory.
2. Check that quotations are copied precisely.
3. Include page numbers for every reference, even if you paraphrase
   or summarize the idea rather than copy it word for word.

A warning about plagiarism

Plagiarism is a form of stealing; as with other offences against the
law, ignorance is no excuse. The way to avoid it is to give credit where
credit is due. If you are using someone else's idea, acknowledge it,
even if you have changed the wording or just summarized the main
points. You may give credit either directly in the text ("As Toynbee
says, . . .") or in a footnote. (For footnote style, see Chapter 14).
Don't be afraid that your work will seem weaker if you acknowledge
the ideas of others. On the contrary, it will be all the more convincing:
serious academic treatises are almost always built on the work of
preceding scholars.

Where should you draw the line on acknowledgements? As a rule
you don't need to give credit for anything that's common knowledge.
You wouldn't footnote the well-known sayings of Jesus, for example,
or lines from "O Canada," or the date of Confederation; however,
you should acknowledge any clever turn of phrase that is neither well
known nor your own. And always document any unfamiliar fact or
claim—statistical or otherwise—or one that's open to question.

Creating an outline

Individual writers differ in their need for a formal plan. Some say that they never have an outline, and others maintain they can't write without one; most fall somewhere in between. Since organization is such a common problem, though, it's a good idea to know how to draw up an effective plan. Of course, the exact form it takes will depend on the pattern you are using to develop your ideas—whether you are defining, classifying, or comparing, for example (see pp. 120-2).

If you have special problems with organizing material, your outline should be formal, in complete sentences. On the other hand, if your mind is naturally logical, you may find it's enough just to jot down a few words on a scrap of paper. For most students, an informal but well-organized outline in point form is the most useful model:

> THESIS: When Trudeau first came to power, his style was seen as an enormous asset, but by the '80s the same style was increasingly seen as a liability.
>
> I. Trudeau's early style perceived in positive light
>   A. Charismatic
>   1. Public adulation: "Trudeaumania"
>   2. Media awe
>   B. Intellectual
>   C. Tough
>   1. Handling of journalists
>   2. Handling of Quebec
>   D. Anti-establishment
>   1. Swinging lifestyle
>   2. Disregard for government traditions
> II. Later reversal: Trudeau's image becomes negative
>   A. Irritating
>   1. Public opinion polls
>   2. Media disenchantment
>   B. Out of touch with economic reality
>   C. Confrontationist
>   1. With individual dissenters
>   2. With Premiers
>   3. With Opposition leaders
>   D. Arrogant
>   1. Extravagant lifestyle in time of recession
>   2. Autocratic approach to governing

The guidelines for this kind of outline are simple:

Code your categories. Use different sets of markings to establish the relative importance of your entries. The example here moves from roman numerals to letters to arabic numbers, but you could use another system.

Categorize according to importance. Make sure that only items of equal value are put in equivalent categories. Give major points more weight than minor ones.

Check lines of connection. Make sure that each of the main categories is directly linked to the central thesis; then see that each subcategory is directly linked to the larger category that contains it. Checking these lines of connection is the best way of preventing essay muddle.

Be consistent. In arranging your points, be consistent. You may choose to move from the most important point to the least important, or vice versa, as long as you follow the same order every time.

Use parallel wording. Phrasing each entry in a similar way will make it easier to be consistent in your presentation.

One final word: be prepared to change your outline at any time in the writing process. An outline is not meant to put an iron clamp on your thinking, but to relieve anxiety about where you're heading. A careful outline prevents frustration and dead ends—that "I'm stuck, where can I go from here?" feeling. But since the very act of writing will usually generate new ideas, you should be ready to modify your original plan. Just remember that any new outline must have the consistency and clear connections required for a unified essay.

THE WRITING STAGE

Writing the first draft

Few writers labour for excellence from scratch; instead, most find it easier to write the first draft as quickly as possible and do extensive revisions later. However you begin, you can't expect the first draft to be the final copy. Skilled writers know that revising is a necessary part of the writing process, and that the care taken with revisions makes the difference between a mediocre essay and a good one.

You don't need to write all parts of the essay in the same order in which they are to appear in the final copy. In fact, many students find the introduction the hardest part to write. If you face the first blank page with a growing sense of paralysis, try leaving the introduction until later, and start with the first idea in your outline. If you feel so intimidated that you haven't even been able to draw up an outline, you might try the approach suggested by John Trimble (1975:11) and charge right ahead with any kind of beginning—even a simple "My first thoughts on this subject are . . . ". Instead of sharpening pencils or running out for a snack, try to get going. Don't worry about grammar or wording; scratch out pages or throw them away if you must. Remember, the object is to get your writing juices flowing.

Of course, you can't expect this kind of exploratory writing to resemble the first draft that follows an outline. You will probably need to do a great deal more changing and reorganizing, but at least you will have the relief of seeing words on a page to work with. Many experienced writers—and not only those with writer's block—find this the most productive way to proceed.

Developing your ideas: some common patterns

The way you develop your ideas will depend on your essay topic, and topics can vary enormously. Even so, most essays follow one or another of a handful of basic organizational patterns. Here's how to use each pattern effectively.

1. Defining

Sometimes a whole essay is an extended definition, explaining the meaning of a term that is complicated, controversial, or simply important to your field of study: for example, *nationalism* in political science, or *monetarism* in economics, or *culture* in anthropology. More often, perhaps, you may want to begin a detailed discussion of a topic by defining a key term, and then shift to a different organizational pattern. In either case, make your definition exact. It should be broad enough to include all the things that belong in the category and at the same time narrow enough to exclude things that don't belong. A good definition builds a kind of verbal fence around a word, herding together all the members of the class and cutting off all outsiders.

For any discussion of a term that goes beyond a bare definition, you should, of course, give concrete illustrations or examples; depending on the nature of your essay, these could vary in length from one or two sentences to several paragraphs or even pages. If you are defining monetarism, for instance, you would probably want to discuss at some length the theories of leading monetarists.

In an extended definition, it's also useful to point out the differences between the term and any other that is connected with it or often confused with it. For instance, if you are defining *deviance* you might want to distinguish it from *criminality*; if you are defining *common law* you might want to distinguish it from *statute law*.

2. Classifying

Classifying means dividing something into its separate parts according to a given principle of selection. The principle or criterion may vary; you could classify kinship, for example, according to whether it is traced through the mother's line or the father's, or both; whether it is by blood or marriage; and whether it includes immediate parent-child (nuclear) or more distant (extended) relations. Members of a given population might be classified according to age group, occupation, income, and so on. If you are organizing your essay by a system of classification, remember the following:

- All members of a class must be accounted for. If any are left over, you need to alter some categories or add more.
- Categories can be divided into subcategories. You should consider using subcategories if there are significant differences within a category. If, for instance, you are classifying the work force according to occupation, you might want to create subcategories according to income level or sex.
- Any subcategory should contain at least two items.

3. Explaining a process

This kind of organization shows how something works or has worked, whether it be the process of urbanization, the process of justice, or the stages in a political or military campaign. The important point to remember is to be systematic, to break down the process into a series of steps or stages. Although at times it may vary, most often your order will be chronological, in which case you should see that the sequence is accurate and easy to follow. Whatever the arrangement, you can generally make the process easier to follow if you start a new paragraph for each new stage.

4. Tracing causes or effects

As we have seen in the first part of this book, tracing causes and effects is at the centre of much social-science research, and it is a complex process. See Chapter 2 for a detailed discussion.

5. Comparing

One point sometimes forgotten is that comparing things means showing differences as well as similarities—even if the topic does not say "compare and contrast." The easiest method for comparison—though not always the best—is to discuss the first subject in the comparison thoroughly and then move on to the second:

Subject *X:*   Point 1
Point 2
Point 3

Subject *Y:*   Point 1
Point 2
Point 3

The problem with this kind of comparison is that it often sounds like two separate essays slapped together. To be successful you must integrate the two subjects, first in your introduction (by putting them both in a single context) and again in your conclusion, where you should bring together the important points you have made about each. When discussing the second subject, try to refer repeatedly to your findings about the first subject ("unlike *X*, *Y* does such and such"). This method may be the wisest choice if the subjects for comparison seem so unlike that it is hard to create similar categories by which to discuss them—if the points you are making about *X* are of a different type than the points you are making about *Y*.

If it is possible to find similar criteria or categories for discussing both subjects, however, the comparison will be more effective if you organize it like this:

Category 1:   Subject *X*
Subject *Y*
Category 2:   Subject *X*
Subject *Y*
Category 3:   Subject *X*
Subject *Y*

Because this kind of comparison is more tightly integrated, the reader can more readily see the similarities and differences between the subjects. As a result, the essay is likely to be more forceful.

Introductions

The beginning of an essay has a dual purpose: to indicate both the topic and your approach to it, and to whet your reader's interest in what you have to say. One effective way of introducing a topic is to place it in a context—to supply a kind of backdrop that will put it in perspective. You step back a pace and discuss the area into which your topic fits, and then gradually lead into your specific field of discussion. Sheridan Baker (1981:24–25) calls this the *funnel approach* (see p. 124 below). For example, suppose that your topic is the industrial development of a particular Third World country. You might begin with a more general discussion of industrialization in the West, and then move on to industrialization in the most advanced Asian and African countries before focusing on your specific topic. A funnel opening is applicable to almost any kind of essay.

It's a good idea to try to catch your reader's interest right from the start—you know from your own reading how a dull beginning can put you off. The fact that your instructor must read on anyway makes no difference. If a reader has to get through thirty or forty similar essays, it's all the more important for yours to stand out. A funnel opening isn't the only way to catch the reader's attention. Here are three of the most common leads:

The quotation. This approach works especially well when the quotation is taken from the person or work that you will be discussing.

The question. A rhetorical question will only annoy the reader if it's commonplace or the answer is obvious, but a thought-provoking question can make a strong opening. Just be sure that you answer the question in your essay.

The anecdote or telling fact. This is the kind of concrete lead that journalists often use to grab their readers' attention. Save it for your least formal essays—and remember that the incident must really highlight the ideas you are going to discuss.

Whatever your lead, it must relate to your topic: never sacrifice relevance for originality. Finally, whether your introduction is one paragraph or several, make sure that by the end of it your reader clearly knows the direction you are taking.

Conclusions

Endings can be painful—sometimes for the reader as much as for the writer. Too often, the feeling that one ought to say something profound and memorable produces the kind of prose that suggests violins throbbing in the background. You know the sort of thing:

> Clearly, Milton Friedman's insight into the operation of Western economies is both intellectually and emotionally stimulating. He has opened broad vistas and forced us to reassess the moral and political underpinnings of economic decision making in the modern world.

Why is this embarrassing? Because it's phony—a grab-bag of clichés.

Experienced editors often say that many articles and essays would be better without their final paragraphs: in other words, when you have finished what you want to say, the only thing to do is stop. This advice works best for short essays, where you need to keep the central point firmly in the foreground and don't need to remind the reader of it. For longer pieces, where you have developed a number of ideas or a complex line of argument, you should provide a sense of closure. Readers welcome an ending that helps to tie the ideas together; they don't like to feel they've been left dangling. And since the final impression is often the most lasting, it's in your interest to finish strongly. Simply restating your thesis or summarizing what you have already said isn't forceful enough. What are the other options?

The inverse funnel. The simplest and most basic conclusion is one that restates the thesis *in different words* and then discusses its implications. Baker (1981) calls this the inverse funnel approach, as opposed to the funnel approach of the opening paragraph.

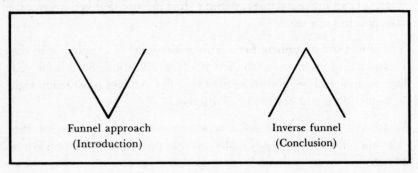

Funnel approach
(Introduction)

Inverse funnel
(Conclusion)

One danger in moving to a wider perspective is that you may try to embrace too much. When a conclusion expands too far it tends to lose focus and turn into an empty cliché, like the conclusion in the preceding example. It's always better to discuss specific implications than to leap into the thin air of vague generalities.

The new angle. A variation of the basic inverse funnel approach is to reintroduce your argument with a new twist. Suggesting some fresh angle can add excitement to your ending. Beware of injecting an entirely new idea, though, or one that's only loosely connected to your original argument: the result could be jarring or even off-topic.

The full circle. If your introduction is based on an anecdote, a question, or a startling fact, you can complete the circle by referring to it again in relation to some of the insights revealed in the main body of your essay.

The stylistic flourish. Some of the most successful conclusions end on a strong stylistic note. Try varying the sentence structure: if most of your sentences are long and complex, make the last one short and punchy, or vice versa. Sometimes you can dramatize your idea with a striking phrase or colourful image. When you are writing your essay, keep your eyes open and your ears tuned for fresh ways of putting things, and save the best for the end.

None of these approaches to endings is exclusive, of course. You may even find that several of them can be combined in a single essay.

THE EDITING STAGE

Often the best writer in a class is not the one who can dash off a fluent first draft, but the one who is the best editor. To edit your work well you need to see it as the reader will; you have to distinguish between what you meant to say and what is actually on the page. For this reason it's a good idea to leave some time between drafts, so that when you begin to edit you will be looking at the writing afresh rather than reviewing it from memory. Now's the time to go to a movie or play some squash—do anything that will take your mind off your work. Without this distancing period you can become so involved that it's hard to see your paper objectively.

Editing doesn't mean simply checking your work for errors in grammar or spelling. It means looking at the piece *as a whole* to see if the ideas are (1) well organized, (2) well documented, and (3) well expressed. It may mean adding some paragraphs, deleting others, and shifting still others around. It very likely means adding, deleting, and shifting sentences and phrases. Experienced writers may be able to check several aspects of their work at the same time, but if you are inexperienced or in doubt about your writing, it's best to look at the organization of the ideas before you tackle sentence structure, diction, style, and documentation.

What follows is a check-list of questions to ask yourself as you begin editing. Far from all-inclusive, it focuses on the first step: examining the organization. You probably won't want to check through your work separately for each question: you can group some together and overlook others, depending on your own strengths and weaknesses as a writer.

Preliminary editing check-list

1. Are the purpose and approach of this essay evident from the beginning?
2. Are all sections of the paper relevant to the topic?
3. Is the organization logical?
4. Are the ideas sufficiently developed? Is there enough evidence, explanation, and illustration?
5. Would an educated person who hasn't read the primary material understand everything I'm saying? Should I clarify some parts or add any explanatory material?
6. In presenting my argument, do I take into account opposing arguments or evidence?
7. Do my paragraph divisions give coherence to my ideas? Do I use them to cluster similar ideas and signal changes of idea?
8. Do any parts of the essay seem disjointed? Should I add more transitional words or logical indicators to make the sequence of ideas easier to follow?

Another approach would be to devise your own check-list based on the faults of previous assignments. This is particularly useful when you move from the overview to the close focus on sentence structure, diction, punctuation, spelling, and style. If you have a particular weak area—for example, irrelevant evidence, faulty logic, or run-on sentences—you should give it special attention. Keeping a personal check-list will save you from repeating the same old mistakes.

A few words about appearance

We've all been told not to judge a book by its cover, but the very warning suggests that we have a natural tendency to do so. Readers of essays find the same thing. A well-typed, visually appealing essay creates a receptive reader and, fairly or unfairly, often gets a higher mark than a hand-written one—especially if the hand-writing is messy or hard to read. Whenever possible, therefore, type your essay. If you can't type or afford to hire a typist, take special care that your script is neat and easy to read. If your hand-writing is poor, print. In any case, double-space your lines and leave wide margins on sides, top, and bottom, framing the script in white. Leave three centimetres at least at the sides and top and four centimetres at the bottom, so that the reader has ample space to write comments. Number each page at the top right-hand corner, and provide a neat, well-spaced cover page which includes the title, your name, and the name of your instructor and course. Good looks won't substitute for good thinking, but they will certainly enhance it.

USING A WORD-PROCESSOR

These days it is becoming more common to see student papers with the characteristic typeface of the dot matrix or — in rare cases — laser printer. The advent of the computer and relatively inexpensive, easy-to-use word-processing packages has made a tremendous difference to the way people write. The word-processor can be a wonderful tool to assist you in your writing — if you use it judiciously.

Using a word-processor does not mean "getting into computers"; most word-processing systems simply make your computer keyboard into a fancy typewriter that allows you to correct mistakes before they arrive on paper, rearrange your material for ease of reading, and print out a neat and tidy final copy. Most systems are easy to learn and they can speed up your writing considerably. To some extent they can also help you to improve your writing skills, because they make it easier for you to revise — to add, delete, or correct, change passages, or move paragraphs around. Here are a few simple suggestions that might be useful if you have, or are thinking of getting, a computer to do word-processing.

1. Type your material directly into the computer

The traditional way of writing a paper that eventually will be typed is to write it out in longhand, and then type it or have someone else type it for you. You can speed up the physical writing process enormously by typing your paper directly into the computer. Even if you can't type very well, it doesn't really matter; when you are writing a paper, the time spent thinking will far outweigh the time it takes to enter the words into the computer. A common argument against writing in this fashion is "I can't think at the typewriter." But once you try, you may find it's rewarding. Seeing your thoughts appearing in a legible form in front of you will help keep you going.

2. Try different ways of organizing your paper

Perhaps the most useful aspect of a word-processing system is that it allows you to move blocks of text around so that you can try out different ways of organizing your paper. If you have ever reached the point where your handwritten version has become so complicated that you have to rewrite the whole thing out in order to make any sense of it, you will appreciate being able to make on-screen corrections and rearrangements. You can set up a new organizational structure for your paper and if, after reading it through, you don't like it, you can always go back to your original version.

3. Don't let the system rule your thinking

Seeing something typed out neatly on a screen or on paper makes it seem more acceptable than messy handwriting, even though the quality of the work may be no different. Don't be fooled into thinking that quality typing replaces quality thinking. Read over your work with a critical eye, in the knowledge that you can easily change something that is unsatisfactory. Remember that the word-processor is a tool for you to use—no more than that.

4. Save regularly and back up your files

If you are used to working with a computer, you know the importance of this advice; if not, take it to heart. There is nothing more agonizing than to discover that something has gone wrong and caused you to lose everything you have been working on. It doesn't happen very often, but everyone experiences it at least once, and always unexpectedly. There is one easy way around the problem: when you are writing, save your work file every fifteen minutes or so. Then when your room-mate pulls the plug on the computer to turn on the TV, the most you will lose is the typing you have done since you last saved your file. A potentially more serious problem may arise if your cat decides to find out what computer disks taste like, or if you are careless with a cup of coffee. Again, a little foresight will save you from losing everything. As soon as you have completed a section of work, make a copy of it on another disk and keep it well away from the computer. An up-to-date back-up system like this will spare you a lot of frustration.

Word-processors are not the answer to all your writing needs, but if you are thinking about getting an electric typewriter, you might consider buying an inexpensive computer instead. It will do a lot more for you—and besides, you can always play video games when the strain of writing becomes too much.

REFERENCES

Baker, Sheridan

1981   *The Practical Stylist*, 5th edition. New York: Harper and Row.

McCrimmon, James

1976   *Writing with a Purpose*, 6th edition. Boston: Houghton Mifflin.

Trimble, John R.

1975   *Writing with Style: Conversations on the Art of Writing*. Englewood Cliffs, N.J.: Prentice-Hall.

9
Writing
a book report

The term *book report* covers a variety of writing assignments, from a simple summary of a book's contents to a complex evaluation. In between is the kind you will most often be asked to produce: an analytic report containing some evaluation. Before you begin your assignment, be sure to check with your instructor to find out exactly which type is expected.

THE INFORMATIVE BOOK REPORT OR SUMMARY

Your purpose in this kind of report is to summarize a book briefly and coherently. It's not a complicated task, but it does call on your ability to get to the heart of things, to separate what is important from what is not—a useful skill both in school and on the job. Aside from some pertinent publication information, all a simple informative report needs is an accurate summary of the book's contents.

Writing guidelines

Determine the author's purpose

An author writes a book for a reason: to cast some new light on a subject, to propose a new theory, or to bring together the existing knowledge in a field. Whatever the purpose, you have to discover it if you want to understand what guided the author's selection and arrangement of material. The best way to find out what the author intends to do is to check the table of contents, preface, and introduction.

Skim-read the book first

As noted earlier (p. 6), a quick overview of the book's contents will show you what the author considers most important and what kind of evidence he or she presents. The details will be much more understandable once you know where the book as a whole is going.

Reread carefully and take notes

A second, more thorough reading will be the basis of your note-taking. Since you have already determined the relative importance that the author gives to various ideas, you can be selective and avoid getting bogged down in a welter of unimportant detail. Just be sure that you don't neglect any crucial passages or controversial claims.

When you are taking notes try to condense the ideas. Don't take them down word for word, and don't simply paraphrase them. You will have a much firmer grasp of the material if you resist the temptation to quote; force yourself to interpret. This approach will also help to make your report concise—remember, you want to be brief as well as clear. Condensing the material as you take notes will ensure that your report is a true summary, not just a string of quotations or paraphrases.

Pull your notes together to form a clear summary of the contents

Give the same relative emphasis to each area that the author does. Don't just list the topics in the book or the conclusions reached: discriminate between primary ideas and secondary ones.

Follow the book's order of presentation. Strictly speaking, a simple summary need not do so, but it's usually safer to follow the author's lead. That way your summary will be a clear reflection of the original.

Follow the logical chain of the arguments. Don't leave any confusing holes. You won't be able to cover every detail, of course, but you must make sure to trace all the main arguments in such a way that they make logical sense.

Include the key evidence supporting the author's arguments. Without some supporting details, your reader will have no way of assessing the strength of the conclusions.

Tailor the length to fit your needs. A summary can be any length, from one page to six or seven. It depends less on the length of the original material than on your purpose. If the report is an assignment, find out how long your instructor wants it to be. If it's for personal reference only, you will have to decide how much detail you want to have on hand.

Read and revise your report to make sure it's coherent

Summaries can often seem choppy or disconnected because so much of the original is left out. Use linking words and phrases (see p. 61) to help create a flow and give your writing a sense of logical development. Careful paragraph division will also help to frame the various sections of the summary.

Include publication details

Details about the book (publisher, place and date of publication, and number of pages) must appear somewhere in your report, whether at the beginning or at the end. Follow the guidelines in Chapter 10. Separate these publication details from your discussion by a triple space.

THE ANALYTIC BOOK REPORT

An analytic book report—sometimes called a book review—not only summarizes the main ideas in a book but at the same time evaluates them. You are best to begin with an introduction, then follow with your summary and evaluation. Publication details can come either at the beginning or at the end.

Introduction

You should provide all the background information necessary for a reader who is not familiar with the book. Here are some of the questions you might consider:

- What is the book about?
- What is the author's purpose? What kind of audience is he or she writing for? How is the topic limited? Is the central theme or argument stated or only implied?
- How does this book relate to others in its special field of interest? To other aspects of the same field?
- What are the author's background and reputation? What other books or articles has he or she written?
- Are there any special circumstances connected with the writing of this book?
- What sources has the author used?

Not all of these questions will be applicable to every book. Nevertheless, an introduction that answers some of them will put your reader in a much better position to appreciate what you have to say.

Summary

Obviously you cannot analyse a book without discussing its contents: the basic steps are the same as for the simple book summary. You may choose to present a condensed version of the book's contents as a separate section, to be followed by your evaluation; or you may prefer to integrate the two, assessing the author's arguments as you present them.

Evaluation

In evaluating the book you will want to consider carefully the points discussed in Chapter 5. In general, keep in mind the following questions:

- How is the book organized? Are the divisions valid? Does the author give short shrift to certain areas? Is anything left out?
- What kind of assumptions does the author make in presenting the material? Are they stated or implied? Are they valid?
- Does the book accomplish what it sets out to do? Does the author's position change in the course of the book? Are there any contradictions or weak spots in the arguments? Does the author recognize those weaknesses or omissions? Remember that your job is not only to analyse the contents of the book, but to indicate its strengths and weaknesses.
- What kind of evidence is presented to support the author's ideas? Is it reliable and up to date? Are any of the data distorted or misinterpreted? Could the same evidence be used to support a different case? Does the book leave out any important evidence that might weaken its case? Is the author's position convincing?
- Does the author agree or disagree with other writers who have dealt with the same material or problem? In what respects?
- Is the book clearly written and interesting to read? Is the writing repetitious? Too detailed? Not detailed enough? Is the style clear? Or is it plodding, or jargonish, or flippant?
- Does the book raise issues that need further exploration? Does it present any challenges or leave unfinished business for the author or other scholars to pick up?
- To what extent would you recommend this book? What effect has it had on you?

10
Writing
examinations

Most students feel nervous before tests and exams. It's not surprising. Writing an essay exam—even the open-book or take-home kind—imposes special pressures because both the time and the questions are restricted: you can't write and rewrite the way you can in a regular essay, and you must often write on topics you would otherwise choose to avoid. And although on the surface objective tests may look easier, because you don't have to compose the answers, they force you to be more decisive about your answers than essay exams do. You know that to do your best you need to feel calm—but how? These general guidelines will help you approach any test or exam with confidence. For special advice on open-book and take-home exams, see pp. 138-9; for objective tests, see p. 139.

Before the exam

Review regularly

A weekly review of lecture notes and texts will help you not only to remember important material but to relate new information to old. If you don't review regularly, at the end of the year you'll be faced with relearning rather than remembering.

Set memory triggers

As you review, condense and focus the material by writing down in the margin key words or phrases that will trigger off a whole set of details in your mind. The trigger might be a concept word that names or points to an important theory or definition, or a quantitative phrase such as "three causes of the decline in manufacturing" or "five reasons for inflation."

Sometimes you can create an acronym or a nonsense sentence that will trigger an otherwise hard-to-remember set of facts—something like the acronym HOMES (Huron, Ontario, Michigan, Erie, Superior) for the Great Lakes. Since the difficulty of memorizing increases with the number of individual items you are trying to remember, any method that will reduce that number will increase your effectiveness.

Ask questions: try the three-C approach

Think of questions that will get to the heart of the material and cause you to examine the relations between various subjects or issues; then figure out how you would answer them. The three-C approach discussed on p. 7 may be a help. For example, reviewing the *components* of the subject could mean focusing on the main parts of an issue or on the definitions of major terms or theories. When reviewing *change* in the subject, you might ask yourself what elements caused it, directly or indirectly. To review *context* you might consider how certain aspects of the subject—issues, theories, actions, results—compare with others on the course. Essentially, what the three-C approach does is force you to look at the material from various perspectives.

Old examinations are useful both for seeing the type of question you might be asked and for checking on the thoroughness of your preparation. If old exams aren't available, you might get together with friends who are taking the same course and ask each other questions. Just remember that the most useful review questions are not the ones that require you to recall facts, but those that force you to analyse, integrate, or evaluate information.

Allow extra time

Give yourself lots of time to get to the exam. Nothing is more nerve-wracking than to think that you're going to be late. If you have to travel, don't forget that traffic can jam, and so can alarm clocks—remember Murphy's Law: "Whatever can go wrong will." Anticipate any unusual difficulties and allow yourself a good margin.

Writing an essay exam
Read the exam

An exam is not a hundred-metre dash; instead of starting to write immediately, take time at the beginning to read through each question and create a plan of action. A few minutes spent on thinking and organizing will bring better results than the same time spent on writing a few more lines.

Apportion your time

Reread the instructions carefully to find out how many questions you must answer and to see if you have any choice. Subtract five minutes or so for the initial planning, then divide the time you have left by the number of questions you have to answer. If possible, allow for a little extra time at the end to reread and edit your work. If the instructions on the exam indicate that not all questions are of equal value, apportion your time accordingly.

Choose your questions

Decide on the questions that you will do and the order in which you will do them. Your answers don't have to be in the same order as the questions. If you think you have lots of time, it's a good idea to place your best answer first, your worst answers in the middle, and your second best answer at the end, in order to leave the reader on a high note. If you think you will be rushed, though, it's wiser to work from best to worst. That way you will be sure to get all the marks you can on your good answers, and you won't have to cut a good answer short at the end.

Keep calm

If your first reaction on reading the exam is "I can't do any of it!" force yourself to keep calm; take ten slow, deep breaths as a deliberate relaxation exercise. Decide which is the question that you can answer best. Even if the exam seems disastrous at first, you can probably find one question that looks manageable: that's the one to begin with. It will get you rolling and increase your confidence. By the time you have finished, you are likely to find that your mind has worked through to the answer for another question.

Read each question carefully

As you turn to each question, read it again carefully and underline all the key words. The wording will probably suggest the number of parts your answer should have; be sure you don't overlook anything (a common mistake when people are nervous). Since the verb used in the question is usually a guide for the approach to take in your answer, it's especially important that you interpret the following terms correctly:

- *explain*: show the how's or why's;
- *compare*: give both similarities and differences—even if the question doesn't say *compare and contrast*;
- *outline*: state simply, without much development of each point (unless specifically asked);
- *discuss*: develop your points in an orderly way, taking into account contrary evidence or ideas.

Make notes

Before you even begin to organize your answer, jot down key ideas and information related to the topic on rough paper or the unlined pages of your answer book. These notes will save you the worry of forgetting something by the time you begin writing. Next, arrange those parts you want to use into a brief plan.

Be direct

Get to the points quickly and illustrate them frequently. In an exam, as opposed to a term paper, it's best to use a direct approach. Don't worry about composing a graceful introduction: simply state the main points that you are going to discuss, then get on with developing them. Remember that your paper will likely be one of many read and marked by someone who has to work quickly—the clearer your answers are, the better they will be received.

For each main point give the kind of specific details that will prove you really know the material. General statements will show you are able to assimilate information, but they need examples to back them up.

Write legibly

Writing that's hard to read produces a cranky reader. When the marker has to struggle to decipher your ideas, you may get poorer results than you deserve. If for some special reason (such as a physical handicap) your writing is hard to read, see if you can make special arrangements to use a typewriter. If your writing is just plain bad, it's probably better to print.

Write on alternate lines

Writing on every other line will not only make your writing easier to read, but leave you space for changes and additions; you won't have to cover your paper with a lot of messy circles and arrows.

Keep to your time plan

Keep to your plan and don't skip any questions. Try to write something on each topic. Remember that it's easier to score half marks for a question you don't know much about than it is to score full marks for one you could write pages on. If you find yourself running out of time on an answer and still haven't finished, summarize the remaining points and go on to the next question. Leave a large space between questions so that you can go back and add more if you have time. If you write a new ending, remember to cross out the old one—neatly.

Reread your answers

No matter how tired or fed up you are, reread your answers at the end, if there's time. Check especially for clarity of expression; try to get rid of confusing sentences and increase the logical connection between your ideas. Revisions that make answers easier to read are always worth the effort.

Writing an open-book exam

If you think that permission to take your books into the exam room is an "Open Sesame" to success, be forewarned. You could fall into the trap of relying too heavily on them; you may spend so much time rifling through pages and looking things up that you won't have time to write good answers. The result may be worse than if you had been allowed no books at all.

If you want to do well, use your books only to check information and look up specific, hard-to-remember details for a topic you already know a good deal about. For instance, if your subject is history you can look up exact dates or quotations; for a political subject you can look up voting statistics; for an exam in social theory you can check some classical references and find the authors' exact definitions of key concepts—if you know where to find them quickly. In other words, use the books to make sure your answers are precise and well illustrated. Never use them to replace studying and careful exam preparation.

Writing a take-home exam

The benefit of a take-home exam is that you have time to plan your answers and to consult your texts or other sources. The catch is that the time is usually less than it would be for an ordinary essay. Don't work yourself into a frenzy trying to respond with a polished research essay for each question; rather, use the extra time to create a well-written exam answer. Keep in mind that you were given this assignment to test your overall command of the course: your reader is likely to be less concerned with your specialized research than with evidence that you have understood and assimilated the material.

The guidelines for a take-home exam are therefore similar to those for a regular exam; the only difference is that you don't need to keep such a close eye on the clock:

1. Keep your introduction short and get to the point quickly.
2. Have a straightforward and obvious organizational pattern so that the reader can easily see your main ideas.
3. Use frequent concrete examples to back up your points.
4. Where possible, show the range of your knowledge of course material by referring to a number of different sources, rather than constantly using the same ones.
5. Try to show that you can analyse and evaluate material: that you can do more than simply repeat information.

Writing an objective test

Objective tests are common in the social sciences. Although sometimes the questions are the true-false kind, most often they are multiple-choice. The main difficulty with these tests is that their questions are designed to confuse the student who is not certain of the correct answers. If you are one of those people who are forever second-guessing themselves, or who readily see two sides to every question, you may find objective tests particularly hard at first. Fortunately, practice almost always improves performance.

Preparation for objective tests is the same as for other kinds. Here, though, it's especially important to pay attention to definitions and unexpected or confusing pieces of information, because they can so readily be adapted to make objective-test questions. Although there is no sure recipe for doing well on an objective test — other than knowing the course material completely and confidently — these suggestions may help you to do better:

Find out the marking system

If marks are based solely on the number of right answers, you should pick an answer for every question even if you aren't sure it's the right one. For a true-false question you have a 50-per-cent chance that it will be; and even for a multiple-choice question with four possible answers, you would get an average of 25 per cent right if you picked the answers blindfolded.

On the other hand, if there is a penalty for wrong answers—if marks are deducted for errors—you should guess only when you are fairly sure you are right, or when you are able to rule out most of the possibilities. Don't make wild guesses.

Do the easy questions first

Go through the test at least twice. On the first round, don't waste time on troublesome questions. Since the questions are usually of equal value, it's best to get all the marks you can on the ones you find easy. You can tackle the more difficult questions on the next round. This approach has two advantages:

1. You won't be forced, because you have run out of time, to leave out any questions that you could easily have answered correctly.
2. When you come back to a difficult question on the second round, you may find that in the meantime you have figured out the answer.

Make your guesses educated ones

If you have decided to guess, at least increase your chance of getting the answers right. Forget about intuition, hunches, and lucky numbers. More important, forget about so-called patterns of correct answers—the idea that if there have been two "A" answers in a row, the next one can't possibly be "A", or that if there hasn't been a "true" for a while, "true" must be a good guess. Unfortunately, many test-setters either don't worry about patterns at all, or else deliberately elude pattern-hunters by giving the right answer the same letter or number several times in a row.

Remember that constructing good objective tests is a special skill that not all instructors have mastered. Often the questions they pose, though sound enough as questions, do not produce enough realistic alternatives for answers. In such cases the test-setter may resort to some less-realistic options, and if you keep your eyes open you can spot them. James F. Shepherd (1979, 1981) has suggested a number of tips that will increase your chances of making the right guess:

- Start by weeding out all the answers you know are wrong, rather than looking for the right one.
- Avoid any terms you don't recognize. Some students are taken in by anything that looks like sophisticated terminology and

may assume that such answers must be correct. They are usually wrong: the unfamiliar term may well be a red herring, especially if it is close in sound to the correct one.

- Avoid extremes. Most often the right answer lies in between. For example, suppose that the options are the numbers 800,000; 350,000; 275,000; and 15: the highest and lowest numbers are likely to be wrong.
- Avoid absolutes, especially on questions dealing with people. Few aspects of human life are as certain as is implied by such words as *everyone*, *all*, or *no one*; *always*, *invariably*, or *never*. Statements containing these words are usually false.
- Avoid jokes or humorous statements.
- Avoid demeaning or insulting statements. Like jokes, these are usually inserted simply to provide a full complement of options.
- Choose the best available answer, even if it is not indisputably true.
- Choose the long answer over the short (it's more likely to contain the detail needed to make it right) and the particular statement over the general (generalizations are usually too sweeping to be true).
- Choose "all of the above" over individual answers. Test-setters know that students with a patchy knowledge of the course material will often fasten on the one fact they know. Only those with a thorough knowledge will recognize that all the answers listed are correct.

Two final tips

If you have time at the end of the exam, go back and reread the questions. One or two wrong answers caused by misreading can make a significant difference to your score. On the other hand, don't start second-guessing yourself and changing a lot of answers at the last minute. Studies have shown that when students make changes they are often wrong. Stick to your decisions unless you know for certain you have made a mistake.

REFERENCES

Shepherd, James F.

1979   *College Study Skills*. Boston: Houghton Mifflin.

1981   *RSVP: The Houghton Mifflin Reading, Study, and Vocabulary Program*. Boston: Houghton Mifflin.

11
Writing with style

Writing with style does not mean stuffing your prose with fancy words and extravagant images. Any style, from the simplest to the most elaborate, can be effective depending on the occasion and intent. Writers known for their style are those who have projected something of their own personality into their writing; we can hear a distinctive voice in what they say. Obviously it takes time to develop a unique style. To begin, you have to decide what general effect you want to create.

Taste in style reflects the times. In earlier centuries, when few people outside the leisured class ever had a chance to read, many respected writers wrote in an elaborate style that we would think much too wordy. Now almost all of us read, but newspapers, television, and radio compete with books for our attention, and as a result we tend to favour a simpler kind of writing. Journalists have led the trend towards short, easy-to-grasp sentences and paragraphs. Writing in an academic context, you may expect your audience to be more reflective than the average newspaper reader, but the most effective style is still one that is clear, concise, and forceful.

BE CLEAR

Since sentence structure is dealt with in Chapter 12, this section will focus on clear wording and paragraphing.

Choose clear words

A good dictionary is a wise investment; get into the habit of using one. It will give you not only common meanings, but less familiar applications, archaic uses, and derivations, as well as proper spelling.

Canadian usage and spelling may follow either British or American practices, but usually combine aspects of both; you should check before you buy a dictionary to be sure that it gives these variants.

A thesaurus lists words that are closely related in meaning. It can help when you want to avoid repeating yourself, or when you are fumbling for a word that's on the tip of your tongue. But be careful: make sure you remember the difference between denotative and connotative meanings. A word's denotation is its primary or "dictionary" meaning. Its connotations are any associations that it may suggest; they may not be as exact as the denotations, but they are part of the impression the word conveys. If you examine a list of "synonyms" in a thesaurus, you will see that even words with similar meanings can have dramatically different connotations. For example, alongside the word *indifferent* your thesaurus may give the following: *neutral, unconcerned, careless, easy-going, unambitious*, and *half-hearted*. Imagine the different impressions you would create if you chose one or the other of those words to complete this sentence: "Questioned about the experiment's chance of success, he was _____ in his response." In order to write clearly, you must remember that a reader may react to the suggestive meaning of a word as much as to its "dictionary" meaning.

Use plain English

Plain words are almost always more forceful than fancy ones. If you aren't sure what plain English is, think of everyday speech: how do you talk to your friends? Many of our most common words—the ones that sound most natural and direct—are short. A good number of them are also among the oldest words in the English language. By contrast, most of the words that English has derived from other languages are longer and more complicated; even after they've been used for centuries, they can still sound artificial. For this reason you should beware of words loaded with prefixes (*pre-, post-, anti-, pro-, sub-, maxi-*, etc.) and suffixes (*-ate, -ize, -tion*, etc.). These Latinate attachments can make individual words more precise and efficient, but putting a lot of them together will make your writing seem dense and hard to understand. In many cases you can substitute a plain word for a fancy one:

Fancy	*Plain*
determinant	cause
utilization	use

cognizant	aware
obviate	prevent
terminate	end
infuriate	anger
oration	speech
conclusion	end
requisite	needed
numerous	many
finalize	finish, complete
systematize	order
sanitize	clean
remuneration	pay
maximization	increase

Suggesting that you write in plain English does not mean that you should never pick an unfamiliar, long, or foreign word: sometimes those words are the only ones that will convey precisely what you mean. Inserting an unusual expression into a passage of plain writing can also be an effective means of catching the reader's attention—as long as you don't do it too often.

Be precise

Always be as precise or exact as you can. Avoid all-purpose adjectives like *major*, *significant*, and *important*, and vague verbs such as *involve, entail*, and *exist*, when you can be more specific:

orig. The survey <u>involved</u> ten questions.

rev. The survey <u>asked respondents</u> ten questions.

Here's another example:

orig. Granting public-service employees the right to strike was a <u>significant</u> legacy of Lester Pearson's years as Prime Minister.

rev. Granting public-service employees the right to strike was a <u>costly</u> legacy of Lester Pearson's years as Prime Minister.

(or)

rev. Granting public-service employees the right to strike was a <u>beneficial</u> legacy of Lester Pearson's years as Prime Minister.

Avoid unnecessary qualifiers

Qualifiers such as *very*, *rather*, and *extremely* are over-used. Experienced writers know that saying something is *very poor* (*rich, weak, strong*, etc.) may have less impact than saying simply that it *is poor* (etc.) For example, compare these sentences:

> Bangla Desh is a poor country.

> Bangla Desh is a very poor country.

Which has more punch?

When you think that an adjective needs qualifying—and sometimes it will—first see if it's possible to change either the adjective or the phrasing. Instead of writing

> The Bank of Montreal made a very big profit last year.

write

> The Bank of Montreal made an unprecedented profit last year.

or (if you aren't sure whether or not the profit actually set a record)

> The Bank of Montreal's profits rose 40 per cent last year.

In some cases qualifiers not only weaken your writing but are redundant, since the adjectives themselves are absolutes. To say that something is *very unique* makes as much—or as little—sense as to say that someone is *rather pregnant* or *very dead*.

Avoid fancy jargon

All academic subjects have their own terminology; it may be unfamiliar to outsiders but it helps specialists to explain things to each other. The trouble is that people sometimes use jargon—special, technical language—unnecessarily, thinking it will make them seem more knowledgeable. Too often the result is not clarity, but complication. The guideline is easy: use specialized terminology only when it's a kind of shorthand that will help you explain something more precisely and efficiently. If plain prose will do just as well, stick to it.

Creating clear paragraphs

Paragraphs come in so many sizes and patterns that no single formula could possibly cover them all. The two basic principles to remember are these: (1) a paragraph is a means of developing and framing an idea or impression, and (2) the divisions between paragraphs aren't random, but indicate a shift in focus.

Develop your ideas

You are not likely to sit down and consciously ask yourself "What pattern shall I use to develop this paragraph? What comes first is the idea you intend to develop: the pattern the paragraph takes should flow from the idea itself and the way you want to discuss or expand it. (The most common ways of developing an idea are outlined on pp. 120-1.)

You may take one or several paragraphs to develop an idea fully. For a definition alone you could write one paragraph or ten, depending on the complexity of the subject and the nature of the assignment. Just remember that ideas need development, and that each new paragraph signals a change in idea.

Consider the topic sentence

Skilled skim-readers know that they can get the general drift of a book simply by reading the first sentence of each paragraph. The reason is that most paragraphs begin by stating the central idea to be developed. If you are writing your essay from a formal plan, you will probably find that each section and subsection will generate the topic sentence for a new paragraph.

Like the thesis statement for the essay as a whole, the topic sentence is not obligatory: in some paragraphs the controlling idea is not stated until the middle or even the end, and in others it is not stated at all but merely implied. Nevertheless, it's a good idea to think out a topic sentence for every paragraph. That way you'll be sure that each one has a readily graspable point and is clearly connected to what comes before and after. When revising your initial draft, check to see that each paragraph is held together by a topic sentence, either stated or implied. If you find that you can't formulate one, you should probably rework the whole paragraph.

Maintain focus

To be clear a paragraph should contain only those details that are in some way related to the central idea. It must also be structured so that the details are easily *seen* to be related. One way of showing these relations is to keep the same grammatical subject in most of the sentences that make up the paragraph. When the grammatical subject is shifting all the time, a paragraph loses focus, as in the following example (based on Cluett & Ahlborn, 1965:51):

orig Boys in school play a variety of sports these days. In the
fall, football still attracts the most, although an increasing
number now play soccer. For some basketball is the favour-
ite when the ball season is over, but you will find that
swimming or gymnastics are also popular. Cold winter
temperatures may allow the school to have an outdoor rink,
and then hockey becomes a source of enjoyment for many.
In spring, though, the rinks begin melting, and so there is
less opportunity to play. Then some boys take up soccer
again, while track and field also attracts many participants.

Here the grammatical subject (underlined) is constantly jumping from
one thing to another. Notice how much stronger the focus becomes
when all the sentences have the same grammatical subject—either
the same noun, a synonym, or a related pronoun:

new · Boys in school play a variety of sports these days. In the
fall, most still choose football, although an increasing
number now play soccer. When the ball season is over,
some turn to basketball; others prefer swimming or gymnastics. If cold winter temperatures permit an outdoor rink,
many boys enjoy hockey. Once the ice begins to melt in
spring, though, they can play less often. Then some take
up soccer again, while others choose track and field.

Naturally it's not always possible to retain the same grammatical
subject throughout a paragraph. If you were comparing the athletic
pursuits of boys and girls, for example, you would have to switch
back and forth between boys and girls as your grammatical subject.
In the same way, you will have to shift when you are discussing examples of an idea or exceptions to it.

Avoid monotony

If most or all of the sentences in your paragraph have the same grammatical subject, how do you avoid boring your reader? There are two
easy ways:

Use stand-in words. Pronouns, either personal (*I, we, you, he, she, it,
they*) or demonstrative (*this, that, those*) can stand in for the subject, as
can synonyms (words or phrases that mean the same thing). The
revised paragraph on boys' sports, for example, uses the pronouns
some, most, and *they* as substitutes for *boys.* Most well-written paragraphs
have a liberal sprinkling of these stand-in words.

"Bury" the subject by putting something in front of it. When the
subject is placed in the middle of the sentence rather than at the

beginning, it's less obvious to the reader. If you take another look at the revised paragraph, you'll see that in several sentences there is a word or phrase in front of the subject, giving the paragraph a feeling of variety. Even a single word, such as *first*, *then*, *lately*, or *moreover*, will do the trick. (Incidentally, this is a useful technique to remember when you are writing a letter of application and want to avoid starting every sentence with *I*.)

Link your ideas

To create coherent paragraphs, you need to link your ideas clearly. Linking words are those connectors—conjunctions and conjunctive adverbs—that show the *relations* between one sentence, or part of a sentence, and another; they're also known as transition words, because they bridge the transition from one thought to another. Make a habit of using linking words when you shift from one grammatical subject or idea to another, whether the shift occurs within a single paragraph or as you move from one paragraph to the next. Here are some of the most common connectors and the logical relations they indicate:

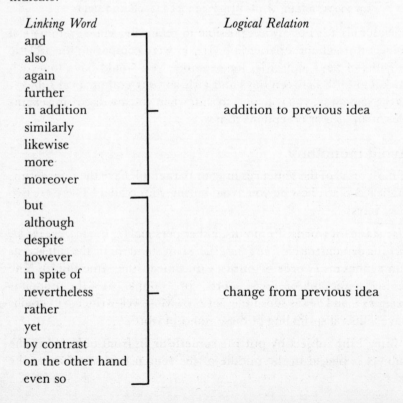

Linking Word	*Logical Relation*
and	
also	
again	
further	
in addition	addition to previous idea
similarly	
likewise	
more	
moreover	
but	
although	
despite	
however	
in spite of	
nevertheless	change from previous idea
rather	
yet	
by contrast	
on the other hand	
even so	

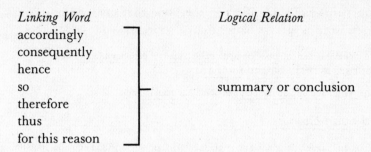

Linking Word	Logical Relation
accordingly	
consequently	
hence	
so	summary or conclusion
therefore	
thus	
for this reason	

Numerical terms such as *first*, *second*, and *third* also work well as links.

Vary the length, but avoid extremes

Ideally, academic writing will have a comfortable balance of long and short paragraphs. Avoid the extremes, especially the one-sentence paragraph, which can only state an idea, without explaining or developing it. A series of very short paragraphs is usually a sign that you have not developed your ideas in enough detail, or that you have started new paragraphs unnecessarily. On the other hand, a succession of long paragraphs can be tiring and difficult to read. In deciding when to start a new paragraph, remember always to consider what is clearest and most helpful for the reader.

BE CONCISE

At one time or another, you will probably be tempted to pad your writing. Whatever the reason—because you need to write two or three thousand words and have only enough to say for one thousand, or just because you think length is strength and hope to get a better mark for the extra—padding is a mistake. You may fool some of the people some of the time, but you are not likely to impress a first-rate mind with second-rate verbiage.

Strong writing is always concise. It leaves out anything that does not serve some communicative or stylistic purpose, in order to say as much as possible in as few words as possible. Concise writing will help you do better on both your essays and your exams.

Guidelines for concise writing

1. Use adverbs and adjectives sparingly

Avoid the shot-gun approach to adverbs and adjectives; don't just spray your work with modifiers in the hope that one will hit. One well-chosen word is always better than a series of synonyms:

orig. As well as being <u>costly</u> and <u>financially extravagant,</u> the venture is <u>reckless</u> and <u>foolhardy.</u>

rev. The venture is <u>foolhardy</u> as well as <u>costly.</u>

2. Avoid noun clusters

A recent trend in some writing is to use nouns as adjectives, as in the phrase *noun cluster*. This device can be effective occasionally, but frequent use can produce a monstrous pile-up of words. Breaking up noun clusters may not always produce fewer words, but it will make your writing easier to read:

orig. word-processor utilization manual
rev. manual for using word-processors

orig. pollution investigation committee
rev. committee to investigate pollution

3. Avoid chains of relative clauses

Sentences full of clauses beginning with *which*, *that*, or *who* are usually more wordy than necessary. Try reducing some of those clauses to phrases or single words:

orig. The solutions <u>which</u> were discussed last night have a practical benefit <u>which</u> is easily grasped by people <u>who</u> have no technical training.

rev. The solutions discussed last night have a practical benefit, easily grasped by non-technical people.

4. Try reducing clauses to phrases or words

Independent clauses can often be reduced by subordination. Here are a few examples:

orig. The report was written in a clear and concise manner and it was widely read.

rev. Written in a clear and concise manner, the report was widely read.

rev. Clear and concise, the report was widely read.

orig. His plan was of a radical nature and was a source of embarrassment to his employer.

rev. His radical plan embarrassed his employer.

For more detail on subordination and reduction, see p. 153.

5. Strike out hackneyed expressions and circumlocutions

Trite or roundabout phrases may flow from your pen without a thought, but they make for stale prose. Unnecessary words are deadwood; be prepared to hunt and chop ruthlessly to keep your writing vital:

Wordy	Revised
due to the fact that	because
at this point in time	now
consensus of opinion	consensus
in the near future	soon
when all is said and done	(omit)
in the eventuality that	if
in all likelihood	likely

6. Avoid "it is" and "there is" beginnings

Although it may not always be possible, try to avoid *it is* or *there is* (*are*) beginnings. Your sentences will be crisper and more concise:

orig. There is little time remaining for the management and employees to reach a settlement before a strike is called.

rev. Little time remains for the management and employees to reach a settlement before a strike is called.

orig. It is certain that crime will increase.

rev. Crime will certainly increase.

BE FORCEFUL

Developing a forceful, vigorous style simply means learning some common tricks of the trade and practising them until they become habit.

Choose active over passive verbs

An active verb creates more energy than a passive one does:

Active: She threw the ball.

Passive: The ball was thrown by her.

Moreover, passive constructions tend to produce awkward, convoluted phrasing. Writers of bureaucratic documents are among the worst offenders:

> It <u>has been decided</u> that the utilization of small rivers in the province for purposes of generating hydro-electric power <u>should be studied</u> by our department and that a report to the Deputy <u>should be made</u> by our Director as soon as possible.

The passive verbs in this mouthful make it hard to tell who is doing what.

Passive verbs are appropriate in two specific cases:

1. When the situation described is in fact passive—that is, when the subject of the sentence is the passive recipient of some action.
2. When using a passive verb will help to maintain focus by eliminating the need to shift to a different subject. The following example has both reasons for using the passive verb *were attacked*:

> The Jesuits began to convert the Hurons, but <u>were attacked</u> by an Iroquois band before they had completed the mission.

Use personal subjects

Most of us find it more interesting to learn about people than about things—hence the enduring appeal of the gossip columns. Wherever possible, therefore, make the subjects of your sentences personal. This trick goes hand-in-hand with use of active verbs. Almost any sentence becomes more lively with active verbs and a personal subject:

orig. The <u>outcome</u> of the union members' vote <u>was</u> the <u>decision</u> to resume work on Monday.

rev. The union <u>members</u> <u>voted</u> to return to work on Monday.

Here's another example:

orig. It <u>can be assumed</u> that an <u>agreement</u> <u>was reached</u>, since <u>there</u> <u>were</u> smiles on both management and union sides when the <u>meeting</u> <u>was finished</u>.

rev. We <u>can assume</u> that management and the union <u>reached</u> an agreement, since both <u>bargainers</u> <u>were smiling</u> when they <u>finished</u> the meeting.

(or)

rev. Apparently <u>management and union</u> <u>reached</u> an agreement since, when <u>they</u> <u>finished</u> the meeting, both <u>bargainers</u> <u>were smiling</u>.

Use concrete details

Concrete details are easier to understand—and to remember—than abstract theories. Whenever you are discussing abstract concepts, therefore, always provide specific examples and illustrations; if you have a choice between a concrete word and an abstract one, choose the concrete. Consider this sentence:

> The French explored the northern territory and traded with the native people.

Now see how a few specific details can bring the facts to life:

> The French voyageurs paddled their way along the river systems of the north, trading their blankets and copper kettles for the Indians' furs.

Suggesting that you add concreteness doesn't mean getting rid of all abstractions. It's simply a plea to balance them with accurate details. Here is one instance in which added wording, if it is concrete and correct, can improve your writing.

Make important ideas stand out

Experienced writers know how to manipulate sentences in order to emphasize certain points. Here are some of their techniques:

Place key words in strategic positions

The positions of emphasis in a sentence are the beginning and, above all, the end. If you want to bring your point home with force, don't put the key words in the middle of the sentence. Save them for the last:

orig · People are less afraid of losing wealth than of losing face in this image-conscious society.

rev · In this image-conscious society, people are less afraid of losing wealth than of losing face.

Subordinate minor ideas

Small children connect incidents with a string of *and*s, as if everything were of equal importance:

> We went to the zoo and we saw a lion and John spilled his drink.

As they grow up, however, they learn to subordinate: that is, to make one part of a sentence less important in order to emphasize another point:

> Because the bus was delayed, we missed our class.

Major ideas stand out more and connections become clearer when minor ideas are subordinated:

orig · Night came and the ship slipped away from her captors.

rev. When night came, the ship slipped away from her captors.

Make your most important idea the subject of the main clause, and try to put it at the end, where it will be most emphatic:

orig · I was relieved when I saw my marks.

rev. When I saw my marks, I was relieved.

Vary sentence structure

As with anything else, variety adds spice to writing. One way of adding variety, which will also make an important idea stand out, is to use a periodic rather than a simple sentence structure.

Most sentences follow the simple pattern of subject—verb—object (plus modifiers):

> The <u>dog</u> <u>bit</u> the <u>man</u> on the ankle.
>   s   v   o

A *simple sentence* such as this gives the main idea at the beginning and therefore creates little tension. A *periodic sentence*, on the other hand, does not give the main clause until the end, following one or more subordinate clauses:

> Since he had failed to keep his promises or to inspire the voters, in the next election <u>he</u> <u>was defeated</u>.
>   s   v

The longer the periodic sentence is, the greater the suspense and the more emphatic the final part. Since this high-tension structure is more difficult to read than the simple sentence, your readers would be exhausted if you used it too often. Save it for those times when you want to create a special effect or play on emotions.

Vary sentence length

A short sentence can add punch to an important point, especially when it comes as a surprise. This technique can be particularly useful for conclusions. Don't overdo it, though. A string of long sentences may be monotonous, but a string of short ones has a staccato effect that can make your writing sound like a child's reader: "This is my dog. See him run."

Use contrast

Just as a jeweller will highlight a diamond by displaying it against dark velvet, so you can highlight an idea by placing it against a contrasting background:

orig. Most employees in industry do not have indexed pensions.

rev. Unlike civil servants, most employees in industry do not have indexed pensions.

Using parallel phrasing will increase the effect of the contrast:

> Although he often spoke to business groups, he seldom spoke in Parliament.

Use a well-placed adverb or correlative construction

Adding an adverb or two can sometimes help you to dramatize a concept:

orig. Although I dislike the proposal, I must accept it as the practical answer.

rev. Athough emotionally I dislike the concept, intellectually I must accept it as the practical answer.

Correlatives such as *both . . . and* or *not only . . . but also* can be used to emphasize combinations as well:

orig. Smith was a good coach and a good friend.

rev. Smith was both a good coach and a good friend.

rev. Smith was not only a good coach but also a good friend.

Use repetition

Repetition is a highly effective emphatic device. It helps to stir the emotions:

> He fought injustice and corruption. He fought complacent politicians and inept policies. He fought hard, but he always fought fairly.

Of course, you would only use such a dramatic technique on rare occasions.

Use your ears

Your ears are probably your best critics: make good use of them. Before producing a final copy of any piece of writing, read it out loud, in a clear voice. The difference between cumbersome and fluent passages will be unmistakable.

Some final advice: write before you revise

No one would expect you to sit down and put all this advice into practice as soon as you start to write. You would feel so constrained that it would be hard to get anything down on paper at all. You will be better off if you begin practising these techniques during the editing process, when you are looking critically at what you have already written. Some experienced writers can combine the creative and critical functions, but most of us find it easier to write a rough draft first, before starting the detailed task of revising.

REFERENCES

Cluett, Robert, and Lee Ahlborn

1965 *Effective English Prose*. New York: L.W. Singer.

12
Common errors in grammar and usage

This chapter is not a comprehensive grammar lesson: it's simply a survey of those areas where students most often make mistakes. It will help you to keep a look-out for weaknesses as you are editing your work. Once you get into the habit of checking, it won't be long before you are correcting potential problems as you write.

The grammatical terms used here are the most simple and familiar ones; if you need to review some of them, see the Glossary. For a thorough treatment of grammar or usage, consult a complete text such as A.J. Thompson and A.V. Martinet's *A Practical English Grammar*, 3rd ed. (Oxford: Oxford University Press, 1980).

Troubles with sentence unity

Sentence fragments

To be complete, a sentence must have both a subject and a verb in an independent clause; if it doesn't, it's a fragment. Occasionally a sentence fragment is acceptable, as in

✓ Will the government try to abolish the Senate? <u>Not likely.</u>

Here the sentence fragment *not likely* is clearly intended to be understood as a short form of *It is not likely that it will try*. Unintentional sentence fragments, on the other hand, usually seem incomplete rather than shortened:

✗ Marx had little respect for capitalism. <u>Being a thinker who opposed exploitation.</u>

The last "sentence" is incomplete: where are the subject and verb? (Remember that a participle such as *being* is a verbal, not a verb; in fact, any *-ing* word by itself is not a verb.) The fragment can be made into a complete sentence by adding a subject and a verb:

> He was a thinker who opposed exploitation.

Alternatively, you could join the fragment to the preceding sentence:

> Being a thinker who opposed exploitation, Marx had little respect for capitalism.

> Marx had little respect for capitalism, since he was a thinker who opposed exploitation.

Run-on sentences

A run-on sentence is one that continues beyond the point where it should have stopped:

> Capitalism is exploitive, but this doesn't stop workers from voting for "establishment" political parties and such is the case in England.

The *and* should be dropped and a period or semicolon added after *parties*.

Another kind of run-on sentence is one in which two independent clauses (phrases that could stand by themselves as sentences) are wrongly joined by a comma:

> C.B. Macpherson has won international acclaim as a political theorist, he is a political-science professor at the University of Toronto.

This error is known as a *comma splice*. There are three ways of correcting it:

• by putting a period after *theorist* and starting a new sentence:

> . . . as a political theorist. He . . .

• by replacing the comma with a semicolon:

> . . . as a political theorist; he

• by making one of the independent clauses subordinate to the other:

> C.B. Macpherson, who has won international acclaim as a political theorist, is a political-science professor at the University of Toronto.

The one exception to the rule that independent clauses cannot be joined by a comma arises when the clauses are very short and arranged in a tight sequence:

> I examined the data, I saw I was on the wrong track, I changed my topic.

Such instances are obviously uncommon.

Contrary to what many people think, words such as *however*, *therefore*, and *thus* cannot be used to join independent clauses:

> ✗ Two of my friends started out in Commerce, however they quickly decided they didn't like accounting.

The mistake can be corrected by beginning a new sentence after *Commerce* or (preferably) by putting a semicolon in the same place:

> ✓ Two of my friends started out in Commerce; however, they quickly decided they didn't like accounting.

The only words that can be used to join independent clauses are the coordinating conjunctions—*and, or, nor, but, for, yet*, and *so*—and subordinating conjunctions such as *if, because, since, while, when, where, after, before*, and *until*.

Faulty predication

When the subject of a sentence is not grammatically connected to what follows (the predicate), the result is *faulty predication*:

> ✗ The <u>reason</u> for his downfall was <u>because</u> he couldn't handle people.

The problem is that *because* essentially means the same thing as *the reason for*. The subject needs a noun clause to complete it:

> ✓ The <u>reason</u> for his downfall was <u>that</u> he couldn't handle people.

Another solution would be to rephrase the sentence:

> ✓ He was defeated because he couldn't handle people.

Faulty *is when* or *is where* constructions can be corrected in the same way:

> ✗ The difficulty <u>is when</u> the two sides disagree.
> ✓ The difficulty <u>arises when</u> the two sides disagree.

Troubles with subject-verb agreement

Identifying the subject

A verb should always agree in number with its subject. Sometimes, however, when the subject does not come at the beginning of the sentence, or when it is separated from the verb by other information, you may be tempted to use a verb form that does not agree:

X   The <u>increase</u> in the rate for freight and passengers <u>were condemned</u> by the farmers.

The subject here is *increase*, not *freight and passengers*; therefore the verb should be the singular *was condemned*:

✓   The <u>increase</u> in the rate for freight and passengers <u>was condemned</u> by the farmers.

Either, neither, each

The indefinite pronouns *either*, *neither*, and *each* always take singular verbs:

X   <u>Neither</u> of the changing rooms <u>have</u> a sauna.

✓   <u>Each</u> of them <u>has</u> a shower.

Compound subjects

When *or*, *either . . . or*, or *neither . . . nor* is used to create a compound subject, the verb should usually agree with the last item in the subject:

✓   <u>Neither</u> of these explanations <u>are</u> complete.
<u>Each</u> of them <u>contains</u> some valid points.

If a singular item follows a plural item, however, a singular verb may sound awkward, and it's better to rephrase the sentence:

orig.   Either my history books or my sociology <u>text</u> <u>is going</u> to gather dust this weekend.

rev.   This weekend, I'm going to leave behind either my history books or my sociology text.

Unlike the word *and*, which creates a compound subject and therefore takes a plural verb, *as well as* or *in addition to* does not create a compound subject; therefore the verb remains singular:

✓   Malinowski <u>and</u> Radcliffe-Brown <u>are</u> classic anthropological thinkers.

✓ Malinowski <u>as well as</u> Radcliffe-Brown <u>is</u> a classic anthropological thinker.

Collective nouns

A collective noun is a singular noun, such as *family*, *army*, or *team*, that includes a number of members. If the noun refers to the members as a unit, it takes a singular verb:

✓ The <u>family</u> <u>goes</u> on holiday in June.

If the noun refers to the members as individuals, however, the verb becomes plural:

✓ The <u>team</u> <u>are receiving</u> their sweaters before the exhibition game.

✓ The <u>majority</u> of immigrants to Canada <u>settle</u> in cities.

Titles

A title is singular even if it contains plural words; therefore it takes a singular verb:

✓ <u>Modern Social Theories</u> was a best-seller.

✓ <u>Marx and Engels</u> is an obvious reference on revolution.

Tense troubles

Native speakers of English usually know the correct sequence of verb tense by ear, but a few tenses can still be confusing.

The past perfect

If the main verb is in the past tense and you want to refer to something before that time, use the past perfect (*had* plus the past participle). The time sequence will not be clear if you use the simple past in both clauses:

X He hoped that she <u>bought</u> the typewriter.

✓ He hoped that she <u>had bought</u> the typewriter.

Similarly, when you are reporting what someone said in the past—that is, when you are using past indirect discourse—you should use the past perfect tense in the clause describing what was said:

X He said that the party <u>caused</u> the neighbours to complain.

✓ He said that the party <u>had caused</u> the neighbours to complain.

Using "if"

When you are describing a possibility in the future, use the present tense in the condition (*if*) clause and the future tense in the consequence clause:

✓ If he tests us on price theory, I will fail.

When the possibility is unlikely, it is conventional—especially in formal writing—to use the subjunctive in the *if* clause, and *would* plus the base verb in the consequence clause:

✓ If he were to cancel the test, I would cheer.

When you are describing a hypothetical instance in the past, use the past subjunctive (it has the same form as the past perfect) in the *if* clause and *would have* plus the past participle for the consequence. A common error is to use *would have* in both clauses:

✗ If she would have been more friendly, I would have asked her to dance.

✓ If she had been more friendly, I would have asked her to dance.

Writing about books

To describe a book in its historical context, use the past tense:

John Porter wrote The Vertical Mosaic at a time when most people believed all Canadians had a good chance at upward mobility.

To discuss what goes on *within* the work, however, you should use the present tense:

Porter sees educational opportunity as important to ordinary Canadians, but not to elites.

When you are discussing an episode or incident in the work and want to refer to a prior or future incident, use past or future tenses accordingly:

The author reminds us that historically immigrants were admitted into Canada to do particular kinds of jobs; today, their descendants will often be prevented from moving into better jobs.

Be sure to return to the present tense when you have finished referring to events in the past or future.

Pronoun troubles

Pronoun reference

The link between a pronoun and the noun it refers to must be clear. If the noun doesn't appear in the same sentence as the pronoun, it should appear in the preceding sentence:

   ✗   The textbook supply in the bookstore had run out, and so we borrowed <u>them</u> from the library.

Since *textbook* is used as an adjective rather than a noun, it cannot serve as referent or antecedent for the pronoun *them*. You must either replace *them* or change the phrase *textbook supply*.

   ✓   The <u>textbook supply</u> in the bookstore had run out, and so we borrowed the <u>texts</u> from the library.

   ✓   The <u>textbooks</u> in the bookstore had run out, and so we borrowed <u>them</u> from the library.

When a sentence contains more than one noun, make sure there is no ambiguity about which noun the pronoun refers to:

   ✗   The public wants increased social <u>services</u> as well as lower <u>taxes,</u> but the government does not advocate <u>them</u>.

What does the pronoun *them* refer to? The taxes, the social services, or both?

   ✓   The public wants <u>increased</u> social <u>services</u> as well as lower taxes, but the government does not advocate such <u>increases</u>.

Using "it" and "this"

Using *it* and *this* without a clear referent can lead to confusion:

   ✗   Although the directors wanted to meet in January, <u>it</u> (<u>this</u>) didn't take place until May.

   ✓   Although the directors wanted to meet in January, <u>the conference</u> didn't take place until May.

Make sure that *it* or *this* clearly refers to a specific noun or pronoun.

Pronoun agreement

A pronoun should agree in number and person with the noun that it refers to:

X   When a Canadian civil <u>servant</u> retires, <u>their</u> pension is indexed.

✓   When a Canadian civil <u>servant</u> retires, <u>his</u> pension is indexed.

Traditionally, the word *his* has been used to indicate both male and female, and most grammarians still maintain that *his* is the correct form. If you feel uncomfortable about using *his* alone, or want to avoid charges of sexism, now and again you may resort to the more cumbersome *his or her*, as this handbook occasionally does. Where possible, though, it's better to try switching from the singular to the plural in both noun and pronoun:

✓   When Canadian civil <u>servants</u> retire, <u>their pensions</u> are indexed.

Whichever form you choose, check for agreement.

Using "one"

People often use the word *one* to avoid over-using *I* in their writing. Although in Britain this is common, in Canada and the United States frequent use of *one* may seem too formal and even a bit pompous:

If <u>one</u> were to apply for the grant, <u>one</u> would find oneself engulfed in so many bureaucratic forms that <u>one's</u> patience would be stretched thin.

As a way out, it's becoming increasingly common in North America to use the third-person *his* or *hers* as the adjectival form of *one* (this doesn't mean that you can use the nominative *he* or *she* for *one* as the subject):

<u>One</u> would find <u>his</u> patience stretched thin.

In any case, try to use *one* sparingly, and don't be afraid of the occasional *I*. The one serious error to avoid is mixing the third person *one* with the second person *you*:

X   When one studies official statistics, you are surprised by their untrustworthiness.

In formal academic writing generally, *you* is not an appropriate substitute for *one*.

Using "me" and other objective pronouns

Remembering that it's wrong to say "Jane and me were invited to the party," rather than "Jane and I were invited," many people use the subjective form of the pronoun even when it should be objective:

X He invited Jane and I to the party.

✓ He invited Jane and me to the party.

The verb *invited* requires an object; *me* is the objective case. The same problem often arises following a preposition:

X Between you and I, Brown is a bore.

✓ Between you and me, Brown is a bore.

X Eating well is a problem for we students.

✓ Eating well is a problem for us students.

There are times, however, when the correct case can sound stiff or awkward:

orig . To whom was the award given?

Rather than keeping to a correct but awkward form, try to reword the sentence:

rev . Who received the award?

Exceptions for pronouns following prepositions

The rule that a pronoun following a preposition takes the objective case has exceptions. When the preposition is followed by a clause, the pronoun should take the case required by its position in the clause:

X The Chairman showed some concern over whom would be selected as Dean.

Although the pronoun follows the preposition *over*, it is also the subject of the verb *would be selected* and therefore requires the subjective case:

✓ The Chairman showed some concern over who would be selected as Dean.

Similarly, when a gerund (a word that acts partly as a noun and partly as a verb) is the subject of a clause, the pronoun that modifies it takes the possessive case:

X Nancy was elated by him winning the presidency.

✓ Nancy was elated by his winning the presidency.

Troubles with modifying

Adjectives modify nouns; adverbs modify verbs, adjectives, and other adverbs. Do not use an adjective to modify a verb:

X He played good. (Adjective with verb)
✓ He played well. (Adverb modifying verb)
✓ He played really well. (Adverb modifying adverb)
✓ He had a good style. (Adjective modifying noun)
✓ He had a really good style. (Adverb modifying adjective)

Squinting modifiers

Remember that clarity largely depends on word order: to avoid confusion, the relations between the different parts of a sentence must be clear. Modifiers should therefore be as close as possible to the words they modify. A *squinting modifier* is one that, because of its position, seems to look in two directions at once:

X She expected in the spring a decline in the stock market.

Was *spring* the time of expectation or the time of the market decline? The logical relation is usually clearest when you place the modifier immediately in front of the element it modifies:

✓ In the spring she expected a decline in the stock market.

✓ She expected a spring decline in the stock market.

Other squinting modifiers can be corrected in the same way:

X Our professor gave a lecture on Marx's Capital, which was well illustrated.

✓ Our professor gave a well-illustrated lecture on Marx's Capital.

Dangling modifiers

Modifiers that have no grammatical connection with anything else in the sentence are said to be *dangling*:

X Walking around the campus in June, the river and trees made a picturesque scene.

Who is doing the walking? Here's another example:

Reflecting on the results of the referendum, it was decided not to press for independence for a while.

Who is doing the reflecting? Clarify the meaning by connecting the dangling modifier to a new subject:

✓ Walking around the campus in June, she thought the river and trees made a picturesque scene.

✓ Reflecting on the results of the referendum, they decided not to press for independence for a while.

Troubles with pairs (and more)

Comparisons

Make sure that your comparisons are complete. The second element in a comparison should be equivalent to the first, whether the equivalence is stated or merely implied:

✗ Today's students have a greater understanding of new technology than their parents.

This sentence suggests that the two things being compared are *technology* and *parents*. Adding a second verb (*have*) equivalent to the first one shows that the two things being compared are *parents' understanding* and *students' understanding*:

✓ Today's students have a greater understanding of new technology than their parents have.

A similar problem arises in the following comparison:

✗ That cabinet minister is a tiresome man and so are his press conferences.

Press conferences may be tiresome, but they are not *a tiresome man*; to make sense, the two parts of the comparison must be parallel:

✓ That cabinet minister is tiresome, and so are his press conferences.

Correlatives (coordinate constructions)

Constructions such as *both . . . and*, *not only . . . but*, and *neither . . . nor* are especially tricky. The coordinating term must not come too early, or else one of the parts that come after will not connect with the common element. For the implied comparison to work, the two parts that come after the coordinating term must be grammatically equivalent:

X He not only understands mainframes but microcomputers too.

✓ He understands not only mainframes but microcomputers too.

Parallel phrasing

A series of items in a sentence should be phrased in parallel wording. Make sure that all the parts of a parallel construction are in fact equal:

X Mackenzie King loved his job, his dogs, and mother.

✓ Mackenzie King loved his job, his dogs, and his mother.

Once you have decided to include the pronoun *his* in the first two elements, the third must have it too.

For clarity as well as stylistic grace, keep similar ideas in similar form:

X He failed Economics and barely passed Statistics, but Political Science was a subject he did well in.

✓ He failed Economics and barely passed Statistics, but did well in Political Science.

REFERENCES

Thompson, A.J., and A.V. Martinet

1980   *A Practical English Grammar*, 3rd edition. Oxford: Oxford University Press.

13
Punctuation

Punctuation causes students so many problems that it deserves a chapter of its own. If your punctuation is faulty, your readers will be confused and may have to backtrack; worse still, they may be tempted to skip over the rough spots. Punctuation marks are the traffic signals of writing; use them with precision to keep readers moving smoothly through your work.

PERIOD [.]

1. Use a period at the end of a sentence. A period indicates a full stop, not just a pause.

2. Use a period with abbreviations. British style omits the period in certain cases, but North American style usually requires it for abbreviated titles (Mrs., Dr., etc.) as well as place-names (B.C., N.W.T., etc.). Although the abbreviations and acronyms for some organizations include periods, the most common ones generally do not (CARE, CIDA, etc.).

3. Use a period at the end of an indirect question. Do *not* use a question mark:

   X He asked if I wanted a substitute?

   ✓ He asked if I wanted a substitute.

COMMA [,]

Commas are the trickiest of all punctuation marks: even the experts differ on when to use them. Most agree, however, that too many commas are as bad as too few, since they make writing choppy and awkward to read. Certainly recent writers use fewer commas than earlier stylists did. Whenever you are in doubt, let clarity be your guide. The most widely accepted conventions are these:

1. Use a comma to separate two independent clauses joined by a coordinating conjunction (and, but, for, or, nor, yet, so). By signalling that there are two clauses, the comma will prevent the reader from confusing the beginning of the second clause with the end of the first:

> ✗ He went out for dinner with his sister and his room-mate joined them later.

> ✓ He went out for dinner with his sister, and his room-mate joined them later.

When the second clause has the same subject as the first, you have the option of omitting both the second subject and the comma:

> ✓ He can understand an argument, but he can't make one himself.

> ✓ He can understand an argument but can't make one himself.

If you mistakenly punctuate two sentences as if they were one, the result will be a *run-on sentence*; if you use a comma but forget the coordinating conjunction, the result will be a *comma splice*:

> ✗ He took his family to the zoo, it was closed for repairs.

> ✓ He took his family to the zoo, but it was closed for repairs.

Remember that words such as *however*, *therefore*, and *thus* are *conjunctive adverbs*, not conjunctions: if you use one of them the way you would use a conjunction, the result will again be a *comma splice*:

> ✗ She was accepted into graduate school, however, she took a year off to earn her tuition.

> ✓ She was accepted into graduate school; however, she took a year off to earn her tuition.

Conjunctive adverbs are often confused with conjunctions. You can distinguish between the two if you remember that a conjunctive adverb's position in a sentence can be changed:

> She was accepted into graduate school; she took a year off, however, to earn her tuition.

Position of a conjunction, on the other hand, is invariable; it must be placed between the two clauses:

> She was accepted into graduate school, but she took a year off to earn her tuition.

When, in rare cases, the independent clauses are short and closely related, they may be joined by a comma alone:

✓ I came, I saw, I conquered.

A *fused sentence* is a run-on sentence in which independent clauses are slapped together with no punctuation at all:

✗ He watched the hockey game all afternoon the only exercise he got was going to the kitchen between periods.

A fused sentence sounds like breathless babbling—and it's a serious error.

2. Use a comma between items in a series. (Place a coordinating conjunction before the last item):

She finally found an apartment that was large, bright, and clean.

Then she had to scrounge around for dishes, pots, cutlery, and a kettle.

The comma before the conjunction is optional:

She kept a cat, a dog and a budgie.

Sometimes, however, the final comma can help to prevent confusion:

When we set off on our trip, we were warned about passport thieves, attacks on single women, and baggage loss.

In this case, the comma prevents the reader from thinking that *attacks* are made on *baggage* as well as *single women*.

3. Use a comma to separate adjectives preceding a noun when they modify the same element:

It was a rainy, windy night.

When the adjectives *do not* modify the same element, however, you should not use a comma:

It was a pleasant winter outing.

Here *winter* modifies *outing*, but *pleasant* modifies the total phrase *winter outing*. A good way of checking whether or not you need a comma is to see if you can reverse the order of the adjectives. If you can reverse it (*rainy, windy night* or *windy, rainy night*), use a comma; if you can't (*winter pleasant outing*), omit the comma.

4. Use commas to set off an interruption (an interrupting word or phrase is technically called a parenthetical element):

✓ The film, I hear, isn't nearly as good as the book.

✓ My tutor, however, couldn't answer the question.

Remember to put commas on *both sides* of the interruption:

✗ The music, they say was adapted from a piece of Mozart.

✓ The music, they say, was adapted from a piece of Mozart.

5. Use commas to set off words or phrases that provide additional but non-essential information:

> Our president, Sue Stephens, does her job well.

> The black retriever, his closest companion, went with him everywhere.

Sue Stephens and *his closest companion* are *appositives*: they give additional information about the nouns they refer to (*president* and *retriever*), but the sentences would be understandable without them. Here's another example:

> My oldest friend, who lives in Halifax, was married last week.

The phrase *who lives in Halifax* is called a *non-restrictive* modifier, because it does not limit the meaning of the word it modifies (*friend*). Without that modifying clause the sentence would still specify who was married. Since the information the clause provides is not necessary to the meaning of the sentence, you must use commas on both sides to set it off.

In contrast, a *restrictive* modifier is one that provides essential information; therefore it must not be set apart from the element it modifies, and commas should not be used:

> The man who came to dinner was my uncle.

Without the clause *who came to dinner*, the reader would not know which man was the uncle.

To avoid confusion, be sure to distinguish carefully between essential and additional information. The difference can be important:

> Students, who are not willing to work, should not receive grants.

> Students who are not willing to work should not receive grants.

6. Use a comma after an introductory phrase when omitting it would cause confusion:

X   On the balcony above the singers entertained the diners.

✓ On the balcony above, the singers entertained the diners.

X When he turned away the prisoner disappeared.

✓ When he turned away, the prisoner disappeared.

7. Use a comma to separate elements in dates and addresses:

> February 2, 1983. (Commas are often omitted if the day comes first: 2 February 1983)
>
> 117 Hudson Drive, Edmonton, Alberta.
>
> They lived in Dartmouth, Nova Scotia.

8. Use a comma before a quotation in a sentence:

> He said, "Life is too short to worry."
>
> "The children's safety," he warned, "is in your hands."

For more formality, you may use a colon (see p. 87).

9. Use a comma with a name followed by a title:

> D. Gunn, Ph.D.
>
> Alice Smith, M.D.

SEMICOLON [;]

1. Use a semicolon to join independent clauses (complete sentences) that are closely related:

> For five days he worked non-stop; by Saturday he was exhausted.
>
> His lecture was confusing; no one could understand the terminology.

A semicolon is especially useful when the second independent clause begins with a conjunctive adverb such as *however, moreover, consequently, nevertheless, in addition*, or *therefore* (usually followed by a comma):

> He bought a bag of doughnuts; however, none of the group was hungry.

Some grammarians may disagree, but it's usually acceptable to follow a semicolon with a coordinating conjunction if the second clause is complicated by other commas:

> John, my cousin, is a keen jogger in all weather; but sometimes, especially in winter, I think it does him more harm than good.

2. Use a semicolon to mark the divisions in a complicated series when individual items themselves need commas. Using a comma to mark the subdivisions and a semicolon to mark the main divisions will help to prevent mix-ups:

> X He invited Prof. Brooks, the vice-principal, Jane Hunter, and John Taylor.

Is the vice-principal a separate person?

> ✓ He invited Prof. Brooks, the vice-principal; Jane Hunter; and John Taylor.

In a case such as this, the elements separated by the semicolon need not be independent clauses.

COLON [:]

A colon indicates that something is to follow.

1. Use a colon before a formal statement or series:

> The winners are the following: Jane, George, and Hugh.

Do not use a colon if the words preceding it do not form a complete sentence:

> X The winners are: Jane, George and Hugh.
> ✓ The winners are Jane, George, and Hugh.

Occasionally, however, a colon is used if the list is arranged vertically:

> The winners are: Jane
>   George
>   Hugh

2. Use a colon for formality before a direct quotation:

> The leaders of the anti-nuclear group repeated their message: "The world needs bread before bombs."

DASH [--]

A dash creates an abrupt pause, emphasizing the words that follow. (Never use dashes as casual substitutes for other punctuation: overuse can detract from the calm, well-reasoned effect you want.)

1. Use a dash to stress a word or phrase:

> The British--as a matter of honour--vowed to retake the islands.

> Foster was well received in the legislature--at first.

2. Use a dash in interrupted or unfinished dialogue:

> "It's a matter--to put it delicately--of personal hygiene."

In typing, use two hyphens together, with no spaces on either side, to show a dash.

EXCLAMATION MARK [!]

An exclamation mark helps to show emotion or feeling. It is usually found in dialogue:

> "Woe is me!" she mourned.

In academic writing, you should use it only in those rare cases when you want to give a point an emotional emphasis:

> He concluded that the dollar would rise in 1985. Some forecast!

QUOTATION MARKS [" " or ' ']

Quotation marks are usually double in American style and single in British. In Canada either is accepted—just be consistent.

1. Use quotation marks to signify direct discourse (the actual words of a speaker):

> I asked, "What is the matter?"

> He said, "I have a pain in my big toe."

2. Use quotation marks to show that words themselves are the issue:

> The term "love" in tennis comes from the French word for "egg."

Alternatively, you may italicize or underline the terms in question.

Sometimes quotation marks are used to mark a slang word or an inappropriate usage, to show that the writer is aware of the difficulty:

> Hitler's "final solution" was the most barbaric act of this century.

Use this device only when necessary; usually it's better to let the context show your attitude, or to choose another term.

3. Use quotation marks to enclose the titles of poems, short stories, paintings, songs, films, and articles in books or journals. In contrast, titles of books, paintings, or music are italicized or underlined:

> The story I like best in Robert Weaver's Canadian Short Stories is "Bernadette" by Mavis Gallant.

4. Use quotation marks to enclose quotations within quotations (single or double depending on your primary style):

> He said, "Hitler's 'final solution' was the most barbaric act of this century."

PLACEMENT OF PUNCTUATION WITH QUOTATION MARKS

Both the British and the American practices are accepted in Canada. British style usually places the punctuation outside the quotation marks, unless it is actually part of the quotation. The American practice, followed in this book, is increasingly common in Canada:

- A comma or period always goes inside the quotation marks:

> He said, "Give me another chance," but I replied, "You've had enough chances."

- A semicolon or colon always goes outside the quotation marks:

> George wants to watch "The Journal"; I'd rather watch the hockey game.

- A question mark, dash, or exclamation mark goes inside quotation marks if it is part of the quotation, but outside if it is not:

> He asked, "What is for dinner?"

> Did he really call the boss a "lily-livered hypocrite"?

> His speech was hardly an appeal for "blood, sweat and tears"!

> I was just whispering to Mary, "That instructor is a--" when suddenly he glanced at me.

• When a reference is given parenthetically (in round brackets) at the end of a quotation, the quotation marks precede the parentheses and the sentence punctuation follows them:

> Lipsey suggests that we should "abandon the Foreign Investment Review Agency" (<u>Globe and Mail</u>, 12 April 1983).

APOSTROPHE [']

The apostrophe forms the possessive case for nouns and some pronouns.

1. **Add an apostrophe followed by "s" to**
   • all singular and plural nouns *not* ending in *s*: *cat's*, *women's*.
   • singular *proper* nouns ending in *s*: *Keats's*, *Sis's* (but note that the final *s* can be omitted if the word has a number of them already and would sound awkward, as in *Jesus'* or certain classical names).
   • indefinite pronouns: *someone's*, *anybody's*, etc.;

2. **Add an apostrophe to plural nouns ending in "s"**: *families'*, *houses'*, *cars'*.

PARENTHESES [( )]

1. **Use parentheses to enclose an explanation, example, or qualification.** Parentheses show that the enclosed material is of incidental importance to the main idea. They make a less pronounced interruption than a dash, but a more pronounced one than a comma:

> My wife (the eldest of five children) is a superb cook and carpenter.

> His latest plan (according to neighbours) is to dam the creek.

Remember that although punctuation should not precede parentheses, it may follow them if required by the sense of the sentence:

> I like coffee in the morning (if it's not instant), but she prefers tea.

If the parenthetical statement comes between two complete sentences, it should be punctuated as a sentence, with the period inside the parentheses:

> I finished my last essay on April 30. (It was on Freud's theory of repression.) Fortunately, I had three weeks left to study for the exam.

2. Use parentheses to enclose references. See Chapters 10 and 11 for details.

BRACKETS [ ]

Brackets are square enclosures, not to be confused with parentheses (which are round).

1. Use brackets to set off a remark of your own within a quotation. They show that the words enclosed are not those of the person quoted:

> Fox maintains, "Obstacles to western unification [in the eighties] are as many as they are serious."

Brackets are sometimes used to enclose *sic* (Latin for *thus*), which is used after an error, such as a misspelling, to show that the mistake was in the original. *Sic* should be underlined:

> The politician, in his letter to constitutents, wrote about "these parlouse [sic] times of economic difficulty."

HYPHEN [-]

1. Use a hyphen if you must divide a word at the end of a line. When a word is too long to fit at the end of a line, it's best to keep it in one piece by starting a new line. If you must divide, however, remember these rules:

- Divide between syllables.
- Never divide a one-syllable word.
- Never leave one letter by itself.
- Divide double consonants except when they come before a suffix, in which case divide before the suffix:

> ar-rangement
> embar-rassment
> fall-ing
> pass-able

When the second consonant has been added to form the suffix, keep it with the suffix:

> refer-ral
> begin-ning

2. Use a hyphen to separate the parts of certain compound words:

> sister-in-law, vice-consul (compound nouns)
>
> test-drive, proof-read (compound verbs)

well-considered plan, twentieth-century attitudes
(compound adjectives used as modifiers preceding nouns)

When you are *not* using such expressions adjectivally, do *not* hyphenate them:

The plan was <u>well considered</u>.
These are attitudes of the <u>twentieth century</u>.

After long-time use, some compound nouns drop the hyphen. When in doubt, check a dictionary.

3. Use a hyphen with certain prefixes (*all-*, *self-*, *ex-*, and those prefixes preceding a proper name):

all-party, self-imposed, ex-jockey, anti-nuclear, pro-Canadian.

4. Use a hyphen to emphasize contrasting prefixes:

The coach agreed to give both <u>pre-</u> and <u>post-game</u> interviews.

5. Use a hyphen to separate written-out compound numbers from one to a hundred and compound fractions used as modifiers:

eighty-one years ago
seven-tenths full

6. Use a hyphen to separate parts of inclusive numbers or dates:

the years 1890-1914
pages 3-40

ELLIPSIS [. . .]
1. Use an ellipsis to show an omission from a quotation:

He reported that "the drought in the thirties, to many farming families in the west . . . resembled a biblical plague, even to the locusts."

If the omission comes at the end of a sentence, the ellipsis is followed by a fourth period.

2. Use an ellipsis to show that a series of numbers continues indefinitely:

1, 3, 5, 7, 9 ...

14
Documentation

Methods of documentation fall into two basic categories: the footnotes-and-bibliography system traditionally used in the humanities and the author-date system used in most scientific writing. Because the social sciences cover such a broad range, and because they often combine elements of both styles (e.g., footnotes as well as author-date citations), this chapter will outline both. Remember, though, that specific formats may vary widely even within a single discipline; always check with your instructor to make sure you are following the preferred practice for each particular subject.

The main reasons for citing outside sources in a paper are to tell readers about other work that has been done on your topic and to let them know where you got your ideas from (if you don't acknowledge your sources, you are committing plagiarism). Thus even though some instructors may be less strict than others about the exact form the documentation takes, all will require that your references be both accurate and complete.

The most direct form of reference, the quotation, is used in every kind of academic writing. Before we consider the specific ways of acknowledging sources, here is a brief guide to incorporating quotations in your own work.

Quotations

Judicious use of quotations can add authority to your writing. But you must use them with care. Never quote a passage just because it sounds impressive; be sure that it really adds to your discussion, either by expressing an idea with special force or cogency, or by giving substance to a debatable point. The guidelines for incorporating quotations are these:

1. Integrate the quotation so that it makes sense in the context of your discussion and fits in grammatically:

✗ Henry Ford had little knowledge of history. "History is bunk," but his opinion is not one that many educated people would accept.

✓ Henry Ford had little knowledge of history. His opinion that "history is bunk" is not one that many educated people would accept.

2. Be accurate. Reproduce the exact wording, punctuation, and spelling of the original, including any errors. You can acknowledge a mistake by inserting the Latin word *sic* in brackets after it (see p. 00). If you want to underline any part of the quotation for emphasis, add *my emphasis* in brackets at the end.

3. If the quotation is no more than four lines long, include it as part of your text, enclosed in quotation marks. A long quotation is usually single-spaced and introduced by a colon. If the first line of the quotation is the beginning of a paragraph, indent the first line an extra three spaces:

> Machiavelli recognized the ability of a republic to change with the times:
>> Therefore, the truth is that a republic is of longer duration and has a much better fortune than a principality, for a republic, by virtue of its diverse citizenry, can better accommodate itself to the changeability of conditions than can a prince.

5. For a quotation within a quotation, use single quotation marks:

> A news report described the scene this way: "When the crowd heard de Gaulle shout, 'Vive le Quebec libre!' they roared with approval."

6. If you want to omit something from the original, use ellipsis marks:

> "The uprising was the result of indifference on the part of national leaders . . . and mismanagement on the part of civil servants."

If the omission is at the end of a sentence, add a fourth period.

7. If you want to insert an explanatory comment of your own into a quotation, enclose it in brackets:

"At private meetings, three western premiers [Bennett, Lougheed, and Devine] strenuously objected to the federal proposal."

DOCUMENTATION IN THE HUMANITIES

The style of documentation followed in the humanities uses footnotes (or endnotes) for references in the text and in bibliography at the end of the paper.

Footnotes

The purpose of footnotes is to allow readers to check sources and verify information, as well as to protect you, the writer, from charges of plagiarism. But too many notes can be distracting for the reader. To avoid clutter, try to include as much as possible of the necessary information in the text itself, and remember that you don't need references to common knowledge or undisputed facts.

Footnotes are used in four specific instances:
- to identify quotations;
- to acknowledge and give exact references to the words or ideas of others—even if you paraphrase or summarize them in your own words;
- to provide additional relevant information or comments that are difficult to fit into the text itself;
- to refer to other parts of a long discussion.

Although you may choose to place all your notes on a separate page at the end of your paper (in which case you may call them *Notes* or *Endnotes*), for readers' convenience they are usually placed at the bottom of the page on which the citation appears. Whichever format you choose, number the notes consecutively and place the corresponding number at the end of the referring sentence; use arabic numerals raised slightly above the line, following all end punctuation. For bottom-of-the-page notes, remember to
- leave a quadruple space between the text and the note;
- indent the note the same number of spaces you use for a paragraph;
- single-space the note and, if you have two or more on a page, leave a double space between them.

The following examples are limited to the most common kinds of footnote and bibliographic references. For more information see the handbook of the Modern Language Association (1977), Turabian (1967), or Wiles (1972).

Format for first references

Book by one author:

> [1]Desmond Morton, Ministers and Generals: Politics and the Canadian Militia (Toronto: Univ. of Toronto Press, 1970), 20.

Capitalize the first letter in the title and subtitle, as well as the first letters of all words except articles, prepositions, and conjunctions. If you give full bibliographic details at the end of the paper, you may omit subtitles in notes. Familiar terms such as *University* or *editor* may be abbreviated.

Book by two authors:

> [2]Craig R. Brown and Ramsay Cook, Canada, 1896–1921:A Nation Transformed (Toronto: McClelland and Stewart, 1976).

Book by three or more authors; edition other than the first:

> [3]Richard G. Lipsey et al., Economics, 4th ed. (New York: Harper and Row, 1982), 67.

Book with one editor:

> [4]Cook, Ramsay, ed. French Canadian Nationalism: An Anthology (Toronto: Macmillan, 1970), 56.

Note that the publisher's name (here, *Macmillan of Canada Ltd.*) need not be given in full.

Book with two editors:

> [5]Ralph Kruyeger and R. Charles Bryfogle, eds., Urban Problems (Toronto: Holt, 1971), 102.

Translation; author's name in title:

> [6]Plato's Republic, G.M.A. Grube, trans. (Indianapolis: Huckett, 1974).

You need not list the author's name when it is part of the title.

Book in more than one volume:

[7]Donald Creighton, John A. Macdonald (Toronto: Macmillan, 1955–56), 2 vols.

Article by one author in a work edited by another:

[8]Michael Hornyansky, "Is Your English Destroying Your Image?" in In the Name of Language, Joseph Gold, ed. (Toronto: Macmillan, 1975).

Article in a journal:

[9]Stephen Kline and William Leiss, "Advertising, Needs and 'Commodity Fetishism'," Canadian Journal of Political and Social Theory 2, no. 1 (Winter 1978), 5–30.

The additions *p.* or *pp.* to indicate page numbers are increasingly omitted from references. Numbers themselves are often contracted to avoid repetition; however, those between *10* and *20* should always be written in full (10-11, 214-18, etc.).

If the issue of the journal in which an article appears is one of several bound together in a single volume with continuous page numbers, you may leave out the week or month of publication. Just give the volume number, year (in parentheses), and page numbers:

[10]George Woodcock, "Anarchist Phases and Personalities," Queen's Quarterly 87 (1980), 82–97.

Unsigned article in an encyclopdeia:

[11]Encyclopaedia Britannica: Micropaedia, 1974 ed., s.v. "Riel, Louis."

When citing entries in dictionaries and other unsigned, alphabetically arranged reference books, use *s.v.* (*sub verbo*, "under the word") rather than volume and page numbers.

When an entry is signed, list the author's name first.

Government document:

[14]Canada Dept. of Labour, Women's Bureau, Changing Patterns in Women's Employment (Ottawa: Queen's Printer, 1966), 70.

Proceedings:

> [15]Canadian Institute of International Affairs, Proceedings
> of Lester B. Pearson Conference on Canada-United States
> Relationship (Niagara-on-the-Lake, Ont.: n.p., 1976), 32.

The abbreviation *n.p.* indicates that there is no publisher.

Book review:

> [16]Grant Reuber, rev. of On Economics and Society by Harry
> G. Johnson, Queen's Quarterly 83, no. 1 (Spring 1976),
> 129–30.

Signed newspaper article:

> [17]Robert Gibbens, "Quebec Government Reviews Equip-
> ment Purchasing Policy," Globe and Mail, Report on Busi-
> ness, 2 Dec. 1982, B3.

Unsigned newspaper article:

> [18]"Financing System Called Damaging to National Growth,"
> Globe and Mail, 14 July 1982, 4.

Format for subsequent references

Subsequent references should usually be brief. In many cases all you
need to note are the author's name and the page number:

> [19]Cook, 95.

If you are citing more than one work by a particular author, however,
you must add the title (it may be in a shortened form) after the author's
name:

> [20]Morton, Ministers and Generals, 22.

Instead of putting subsequent references as footnotes, you may
enclose them in parentheses and include them in the body of the text,
before the closing punctuation in the referring sentence:

> Educators can also be trendy; the charge may be fair that
> those who deplore a return to the basics are "suffering from
> delirium trendens" (Hornyansky, 93).

If you are repeatedly referring to a single primary source, in references
after the first you may simply enclose the page numbers in parentheses.

Bibliographies

A bibliography is an alphabetical list of both the works cited in a paper and those found useful in preparing it. Your instructor may not require a bibliography if all your references are fully documented in footnotes, but it's a good idea to provide one anyway.

The format for bibliographies differs slightly from that for footnotes:

1. Use a separate page at the end of your paper with the heading *Bibliography* centred on the page.
2. Instead of numbering the entries, list them alphabetically by the author's or editor's surname. If no author is given, begin with the first significant word in the title.
3. Begin each entry at the margin and indent subsequent lines five spaces.
4. Single-space each entry, leaving a double space between entries.
5. Separate the main divisions in each entry with periods rather than commas and parentheses.

Book:

> Fox, Paul W., ed. Politics: Canada. 4th ed. Toronto: McGraw-Hill Ryerson, 1977.

If you include more than one work by a particular author, place the entries in alphabetical order by title (not counting initial articles). List the author's name in the first entry only. For subsequent entries, type ten hyphens and a period; then leave two spaces and give the next title:

> Laxer, James. Canada's Economic Strategy. Toronto: McClelland and Stewart, 1981.
> ---------. Canada's Energy Crisis. Toronto: Lorimer, 1975.

If there is more than one author or editor, use inverted order for the first name only and natural order for the rest:

> Brown, Craig R. and Ramsay Cook. Canada: 1896–1921: A Nation Transformed. Toronto: McClelland and Stewart, 1976.

Article in a book:

> Ward, Barbara. "The First National Nation." In Canada: A Guide to the Peaceable Kingdom, 45–9. William Kilbourn, ed. Toronto: Macmillan, 1970.

Article in a journal:

> Kline, Stephen, and William Leiss. "Advertising, Needs and
> 'Commodity Fetishism'." Canadian Journal of Political and
> Social Theory 2, no. 1 (Winter 1978), 5–30.

DOCUMENTATION IN THE SCIENCES

The rules regarding plagiarism are the same for the sciences as for
the humanities. However, the methods of documentation differ in
two important ways:
- Instead of footnotes, you use brief references, called *citations*,
  in the text itself to acknowledge sources (although you may use
  footnotes as well for additional comments).
- Instead of a bibliography, you use a section entitled *References*
  (or *Literature Cited*) in which you list only those works that you
  refer to directly in the text; other works are not listed.

Although there are two main styles of citation in scientific writing,
alphabetical and consecutive, we will consider only the first. But even
here the specific formats can vary greatly. The model for our outline
(and for references throughout this book) is the *Canadian Journal of
Sociology*. Ask your instructor to recommend a journal that you can
use as a model for each particular course.

Citation in the text

The variable elements in citation style include punctuation, spacing,
and the use of abbreviations and italics (or underlining). So keep in
mind that that the following guidelines are only that: a set of general
principles that will help you make sure that your references include
all the necessary information.

1. Insert the author's name and the date of publication into the
   text at the appropriate point:

   The study by Smith (1983) shows . . .

   Similar studies (Black, 1983; Jones, 1984) also suggest . . .

2. If there are two authors, always cite both names each time you
   refer to the work:

   Peters and Waterman (1984) defined excellence as continued
   massive profitability.

A recent study found that "excellent" business organizations shared a number of features in common (Peters and Waterman, 1984).

3. If there are more than two authors, give the name of the first author only, followed by *et al.*:

The study by Jencks et al. (1972) showed that the amount of unpredictability was greater than that of predictability.

4. If you cite more than one item within a single set of parentheses, arrange them as follows:

- several papers by one author ordered chronologically:

(Smith, 1969, 1973, 1980, in press)

- several papers by the same author in the same year ordered with letter suffixes after the year:

(Black, 1982a, 1982b)

- several papers by different authors in alphabetical order:

(Black, 1982a; Jones, 1984; Smith, 1983)

5. If you are referring to a particular part of a source, always give the specific location (page, figure, or table numbers):

(Smith, 1983:45)

(Jones, 1984:Figure 2.1)

6. Although in general you should cite only those works that you have read, occasionally you may need to include something you have only seen referred to elsewhere. In that case, cite the work in which you found the reference by adding a note to your citation:

(Brown, 1979, as cited in Smith, 1982a:67)

Citation in the Reference section

Although sources are always cited in alphabetic order in the Reference section, we urge you to keep in mind that specific details vary greatly. Always consult a journal in your field for an appropriate model. Here are the general guidelines:

1. List references alphabetically, by the first author's surname.
2. If there are two authors, list the second name in natural order.

3. If there are more than two authors, you may or may not be required to list all the names; our model relies on *et al.*
4. When citing more than one work by a particular author, list them in chronological order, using letter suffixes as necessary.
5. When citing an article in journal, always give the volume and page numbers.

Book:

Peters, Thomas J., and Robert H. Waterman, Jr.
1984   In Search of Excellence: Lessons from America's
Best-Run Companies. New York: Warner Books.

Journal:

Bales, Robert F.
1950   "A set of categories for the analysis of small group
interaction," American Sociological Review
15:257-263.

REFERENCES

Modern Language Association

1977   *MLA Handbook for Writers of Research Papers, Theses, and Dissertations.*
New York: Modern Language Association.

Turabian, Kate

1967   *A Manual for Writers of Term Papers, Theses, and Dissertations*, 3rd
edition, revised. Chicago: University of Chicago Press.

Wiles, Roy

1972   *Scholarly Reporting in the Humanities.* Toronto: University of Toronto
Press.

CATCHLIST
of misused words
and phrases

accept, except. **Accept** is a verb meaning to *receive affirmatively*; **except,** when used as a verb, means to *exclude*:

> I accept your offer.
> The teacher excepted him from the general punishment.

accompanied by, accompanied with. Use **accompanied by** for people; **accompanied with** for objects:

> He was accompanied by his wife.
> The brochure arrived, accompanied with a discount coupon.

advice, advise. **Advice** is a noun, **advise** a verb:

> He was advised to ignore the others' advice.

affect, effect. As a verb to **affect** means to *influence*; as a noun it's a technical psychological term. The verb to **effect** means to *bring about*. The noun means *result*. In most cases, you will be safe if you remember to use **affect** for the verb and **effect** for the noun:

> The eye drops affect his vision.
> The effect of higher government spending is higher inflation.

all together, altogether. **All together** means *in a group*; **altogether** is an adverb meaning *entirely*:

> He was altogether certain that the children were all together.

alot. Write as two separate words: *a lot.*

allusion, illusion. An **allusion** is an indirect reference to something; an **illusion** is a false perception:

> The "double ghetto" is an allusion to the traditional exclusion of Jews from ordinary jobs.

He thought women's opportunities were improving, but it was an illusion.

among, between. Use **among** for three or more persons or objects, **between** for two:

Between you and me, there's trouble among the team members.

amoral, immoral. Amoral means *non-moral* or outside the moral sphere; **immoral** means *wicked*:

As an art critic, he was amoral in his judgements.
That immoral performance should be restricted to adults.

amount, number. Use **amount** for money or noncountable quantities; use **number** for countable items:

No amount of wealth or number of expensive possessions will make up for a lack of love.

anyways. Non-standard English: use *anyway*.

as, because. As is a weaker conjunction than **because** and may be confused with *when*:

As I was working, I ate at my desk.
Because I was working, I ate at my desk.

He arrived as I was leaving.
He arrived when I was leaving.

as to. A common feature of bureaucratese; replace it with a single-word preposition such as *about* or *on*:

X They were concerned as to the range of disagreement.
✓ They were concerned about the range of disagreement.

X They recorded his comments as to the treaty.
✓ They recorded his comments on the treaty.

bad, badly. Bad is an adjective meaning *not good*:

The meat tastes bad.
He felt bad about forgetting the dinner party.

Badly is an adverb meaning *not well;* when used with the verbs **want** or **need**, it means *very much*:

She thought he played the villain's part badly.
I badly need a new suit.

beside, besides. Beside is a preposition meaning *next to*:

> She worked <u>beside</u> her assistant.

Besides has two uses: as a preposition it means *in addition to*; as a conjunctive adverb it means *moreover*:

> <u>Besides</u> recommending the changes, the consultants are implementing them.
> <u>Besides,</u> it was hot and we wanted to rest.

between. See **among**.

bring, take. One **brings** something to a closer place and **takes** it to a farther one.

can, may. Can means to *be able*; **may** means to *have permission*:

> <u>Can</u> you fix the lock?
> <u>May</u> I have another piece of cake?

In speech, **can** is used to cover both meanings: in formal writing, however, you should observe the distinction.

can't hardly. A faulty combination of the phrases **can't** and **can hardly**. Use one or the other of them instead:

> He <u>can't</u> swim.
> He <u>can hardly</u> swim.

capital, capitol. As a noun **capital** may refer to a seat of government, the top of a pillar, an upper-case letter, or accumulated wealth. **Capitol** refers only to a specific American—or ancient Roman—legislative building.

complement, compliment. The verb to **complement** means to *complete*; to **compliment** means to *praise*:

> His skill in data analysis complements the skills of the theorists.

continual, continuous. Continual means *repeated over a period of time*; **continuous** means *constant* or *without interruption*:

> The strikes caused <u>continual</u> delays in building the road.
> In August, it rained <u>continuously</u> for five days.

could of. Incorrect, as are **might of, should of,** and **would of.** Replace **of** with *have*:

- ✗ He <u>could of</u> done it.
- ✓ He <u>could have</u> done it.
- ✓ They <u>might have</u> been there.
- ✓ I <u>should have</u> known.
- ✓ We <u>would have</u> left earlier.

council, counsel. Council is a noun meaning an *advisory* or *deliberative assembly*. **Counsel** as a noun means *advice* or *lawyer*; as a verb it means to *give advice*:

> The college <u>council</u> meets on Tuesday.
> We respect his <u>counsel</u>, since he's seldom wrong.
> As a camp <u>counsellor</u>, you may need to <u>counsel</u> parents as well as children.

criterion, criteria. A **criterion** is a standard for judging something. **Criteria** is the plural of **criterion** and thus requires a plural verb:

> <u>These</u> are my <u>criteria</u> for selecting the paintings.

data. The plural of *datum*, **data** is increasingly treated as a singular noun, but this usage is not yet acceptable in formal prose: use a plural verb.

different than. Incorrect. Use either **different from** (American usage) or **different to** (British).

disinterested, uninterested. Disinterested implies impartiality or neutrality; **uninterested** implies a lack of interest:

> As a <u>disinterested</u> observer, he was in a good position to judge the issue fairly.
> <u>Uninterested</u> in the proceedings, he yawned repeatedly.

due to. Although increasingly used to mean *because of*, **due** is an adjective and therefore needs to modify something:

- ✗ Due to his impatience, we lost the contract. [<u>Due</u> is dangling]
- ✓ The loss was <u>due to</u> his impatience.

farther, further. Farther refers to distance, **further** to extent:

> He paddled <u>farther</u> than his friends.
> He explained the plan <u>further</u>.

good, well. Good is an adjective, not an adverb. **Well** can be both: as an adverb, it means *effectively*; as an adjective, it means *healthy*:

> The pear sauce tastes good.
> She is a good golfer.
> She plays golf well.
> At last, he is well again after his long bout of flu.

hanged, hung. Hanged means *executed by hanging*. **Hung** means *suspended* or *clung to*:

> He was hanged at dawn for the murder.
> He hung the picture.
> He hung to the boat when it capsized.

hopefully. Use **hopefully** as an adverb meaning *full of hope*:

> She scanned the horizon hopefully, waiting for her friend's ship to appear.

In formal writing, using **hopefully** to mean *I hope* is still frowned upon, although increasingly common; it's better to use *I hope*:

> ✗ Hopefully we'll make a bigger profit this year.
> ✓ I hope we'll make a bigger profit this year.

imply, infer. Imply refers to what a statement suggests; **infer** relates to the audience's interpretation:

> His letter implied that he was lonely.
> I inferred from his letter that he would welcome a visit.

irregardless. Redundant; use *regardless*.

its, it's. Its is a form of possessive pronoun; **it's** is a contraction of *it is*. Many people mistakenly put an apostrophe in **its** in order to show possession:

> ✗ The cub wanted it's mother.
> ✓ The cub wanted its mother.
> ✓ It's time to leave.

less, fewer. Use **less** for money and things that are not countable; use **fewer** for things that are:

> Now that he's earning less money he's going to fewer movies.

lie, lay. To **lie** means to *assume a horizontal position*; to **lay** means to *put down*. The changes of tense often cause confusion:

Present	Past	Past participle
lie	lay	lain
lay	laid	laid

like, as. **Like** is a preposition, but it is often wrongly used as a conjunction. To join two independent clauses, use the conjunction **as**:

X I want to progress <u>like</u> you have this year.
✓ I want to progress <u>as</u> you have this year.

✓ Prof. Dodd is <u>like</u> my old school principal.

might of. See **could of.**

myself, me. **Myself** is an intensifier of, not a substitute for, *I* or *me*:

X He gave it to John and <u>myself</u>.
✓ He gave it to John and <u>me</u>.

X Jane and <u>myself</u> are invited.
✓ Jane and <u>I</u> are invited.

✓ <u>Myself</u>, I would prefer a swivel chair.

nor, or. Use **nor** with **neither** and **or** by itself or with **either**:

He is <u>neither</u> overworked <u>nor</u> underfed.
The plant is <u>either</u> diseased <u>or</u> dried out.

off of. Remove the unnecessary **of**:

X The fence kept the children <u>off of</u> the premises.
✓ The fence kept the children <u>off</u> the premises.

phenomenon. A singular noun: the plural is **phenomena**.

principal, principle. As an adjective, **principal** means *main* or *most important*; a **principal** is the head of a school. A **principle** is a *law* or *controlling idea*:

Our <u>principal</u> aim is to reduce the deficit.
Our <u>principal</u>, Prof. Smart, retires next year.
We are defending the preferential hiring of Canadians as a matter of <u>principle</u>.

rational, rationale. **Rational** is an adjective meaning *logical* or *able to reason*. **Rationale** is a noun meaning *explanation*:

That was not a <u>rational</u> decision.
The president sent around a memo with a <u>rationale</u> for his proposal.

real, really. The adjective **real** should never be used as an adverb; use *really* instead:

✓ We had real maple syrup with our pancakes.

✗ It was real good.

✓ It was really good.

set, sit. To **sit** means to *rest on the buttocks*; to **set** means to *put* or *place*:

After standing so long, you'll want to sit down.
Please set the bowl on the table.

should of. See **could of.**

their, there. **Their** is the possessive form of the third person plural pronoun. **There** is usually an adverb, meaning *at that place* or *at that point*; sometimes it is used as an expletive (an introductory word in a sentence):

They parked their bikes there.
There is no point in arguing with you.

to, too, two. **To** is a preposition, as well as part of the infinitive form of a verb:

We went to town in order to shop.

Too is an adjective showing degree (the soup is *too* hot) or an adverb meaning *moreover*. **Two** is the spelled version of the number 2.

while. To avoid misreadings, use **while** only when you mean *at the same time that*. Do not use it as a substitute for *although*, *whereas*, or *but*:

✗ While he's getting fair marks, he'd like to do better.

✗ I headed for home, while she decided to stay.

✓ He fell asleep while he was reading.

-wise. Never use **-wise** as a suffix to form new words when you mean *with regard to*:

✗ Sales-wise, the company did better last year.

✓ With regard to sales, the company did better last year.

(or) The company's sales increased last year.

your, you're. **Your** is a pronominal adjective used to show possession; **you're** is a contraction of *you are*:

You're likely to miss your train.

Glossary I: social science

actual (intervention)
an action or program aimed at changing an existing social condition.

anomaly
a finding that does not fit the thinking within a paradigm.

applied research
research intended to provide decision-makers with practical, action-oriented recommendations to solve a problem.

authority
a highly regarded scholar, reference to whom is used to support a line of argument.

basic research
research intended to make and test theories about some aspect of reality.

bias
see researcher bias.

constant
a characteristic (of a person, group, or society) that does not change over time.

construct (validity)
a high degree of correlation among items believed to measure the same thing.

data
facts or evidence, based on observation, experience, or experimentation, that can be checked or verified.

dependent (variable)
a characteristic or condition that results from change in another characteristic or condition; a variable assumed to be the effect of an independent variable.

disconfirmatory (finding)
an observed relationship that fails to prove a hypothesis correct.

experiment
a study of groups or individuals carried out in an environment controlled by the researcher, who manipulates some variables to see their effects on others.

face (validity)
the accuracy with which an indicator appears to measure the variable it is meant to represent.

hypothesis
a statement of an expected relationship between two or more variables.

imagined (intervention)
an action or program, imagined but not carried out, that would aim at changing an existing social condition.

independent (variable)
a causal or explanatory variable presumed to cause changes in the dependent variable.

intervening (variable)
a variable through which the independent variable acts on the dependent variable.

intervention
an action or manipulation whose effect on a group of people is to be studied.

model
a theoretical "picture" of the relations among causes and effects.

negative (relationship)
a relationship between two variables, in which an increase in one produces a decrease in the other.

ordinal (measure)
the level or type of measurement that arrays (or "orders") people from most to least in respect to some characteristic.

operationalize
devise measures to accurately represent concepts or variables in a theory.

paradigm
a theoretical perspective or way of viewing the world.

policy instrument (or policy tool)
an organizational resource (e.g., the right to legislate and enforce a policy) that can be used to influence social problems.

policy research
see **applied research**.

positive (relationship)
a relationship between variables, in which an increase in one produces an increase in the other.

pure research
see **basic research**.

qualitative (data)
data that cannot be satisfactorily described by numbers and must be described in words.

quantitative (data)
data that can be satisfactorily described by numbers.

quasi-experiment
a modified experiment in which the experimenter cannot exercise complete control over sampling or the research environment.

reactivity
a condition under which subjects behave differently from usual because they are aware they are being studied.

relationship
an association or connection between variables, such that a change in one produces a change in the other.

reliability
the extent to which a measuring procedure produces consistent results over time or with different investigators.

researcher bias
the effect of a researcher's beliefs or expectations on the findings of a study.

scale
a set of measured items combined to provide a single overall measure of some concept or variable.

significance (statistical)
the likelihood that an observed relationship has occurred by chance alone.

strong (relationship)
a relationship between variables, in which a large change in one variable produces a large change in the other.

test (verify)
examine the correctness of a theory by matching predicted against observed findings.

theory
a set of interconnected statements or propositions that explains a causal relationship.

unobtrusive (measure)
any data-collection method that does not make subjects aware of being studied and therefore does not change their behaviour.

validity
the ability of an indicator or measure to accurately represent the variable it is meant to represent.

value neutrality
a way of proceeding in research that seeks to ensure a fair hearing for what the data actually show.

variable
a characteristic or condition that can differ from one person, group, or situation to another.

verify (validate)
see test.

weak (relationship)
a relationship between variables, in which a large change in one variable produces a small change in the other.

Glossary II: grammar

abstract
a summary accompanying a formal scientific report or paper, briefly outlining the contents.

abstract language
theoretical language removed from concrete particulars: e.g., *justice, goodness, truth* (cf. **concrete language**).

acronym
a word made up of the first letters of a group of words: e.g., *NATO* for *North Atlantic Treaty Organization.*

active voice
see **voice**.

adjective
a word that modifies or describes a noun or pronoun, hence a kind of noun marker: e.g., *red, beautiful, solemn.* An **adjectival phrase** or **adjectival clause** is a group of words modifying a noun or pronoun.

adverb
a word that modifies or qualifies a verb, adjective, or adverb, often answering a question such as *how? why? when?* or *where?*: e.g., *slowly, fortunately, early, abroad.* An **adverbial phrase** or **adverbial clause** is a group of words modifying a verb, adjective, or adverb: e.g., *by force, in revenge.* See also **conjunctive adverb**.

agreement
consistency in tense, number, or person between related parts of a sentence: e.g., between subject and verb, or noun and related pronoun.

ambiguity
vague or equivocal language; meaning that can be taken two ways.

antecedent (referent)
the noun for which a pronoun stands.

appositive
a word or phrase that identifies a preceding noun or pronoun: e.g., *Mrs. Jones,* **my aunt,** *is sick.* The second phrase is said to be *in apposition* to the first.

article
a word that precedes a noun and shows whether the noun is definite or indefinite; a kind of determiner or noun-marker. **Indefinite article:** *a (an).* **Definite article:** *the.*

assertion
a positive statement or claim: e.g., *The Senate is irrelevant.*

auxiliary
a verb used in combination with another verb to create a verb phrase; a helping verb used to create certain tenses and emphases: e.g., *could, do, may, will, have.*

bibliography
(a) a list of works referred to or found useful in the preparation of an essay or report; (b) a reference book listing works available in a particular subject.

case
the inflected form of pronouns (see **inflection**). **Subjective case**: *I, we, he, she, it, they*. **Objective case**: *me, us, him, her, it, them*. **Possessive case**: *my , our, his, her, its, their*.

circumlocution
a roundabout or circuitous expression: e.g., *in a family way* for *pregnant*; *at this point in time* for *now*.

clause
a group of words containing a subject and predicate. An **independent clause** can stand by itself as a complete sentence: e.g., *I bought a hamburger*. A **subordinate** or **dependent clause** cannot stand by itself but must be connected to another clause: e.g., **Since I was hungry**, *I bought a hamburger*.

cliché
a trite or well-worn expression that has lost its impact through overuse: e.g., *slept like a log, sunny disposition, tried and true*.

collective noun
a noun that is singular in form but refers to a group: e.g., *family, team, jury*. It may take either a singular or a plural verb, depending on whether it refers to individual members or to the group as a whole.

comma splice
see **run-on sentence**.

complement
a completing word or phrase that usually follows a linking verb to form a **subjective** complement: e.g., (1) *He is* **my father**. (2) *That cigar smells* **terrible**. If the complement is an adjective it is sometimes called a **predicate adjective**. An **objective complement** completes the direct object rather than the subject: e.g., *We found him* **honest and trustworthy**.

complex sentence
a sentence containing a dependent clause as well as an independent one: e.g., *I bought the ring, although it was expensive*.

compound sentence
a sentence containing two or more independent clauses: e.g., *I saw the car wreck and I reported it*. A sentence is called **compound-complex** if it contains a dependent clause as well as two independent ones: e.g., *When the fog lifted, I saw the car wreck and I reported it*.

conclusion
the part of an essay in which the findings are pulled together or implications revealed so that the reader has a sense of closure or completion. In a business report the conclusion is sometimes placed at the front.

concrete language
specific language, giving particular details (often details of sense): e.g., *red, corduroy dress, three long-stemmed roses* (cf. **abstract language**).

conjunction

an uninflected word used to link words, phrases, or clauses. A **coordinating conjunction** (e.g., *and, or, but, for, yet*) links two equal parts of a sentence. A **subordinating conjunction**, placed at the beginning of a subordinate clause, shows the logical dependence of that clause on another: e.g., (1) **Although** *I am poor, I am happy.* (2) **While** *others slept, he studied.* **Correlative conjunctions** are pairs of coordinating conjunctions (see **correlatives**).

conjunctive adverb

a type of adverb that shows the logical relation between the phrase or clause that it modifies and a preceding one: e.g., (1) *I sent the letter; it never arrived,* **however**. (2) *The battery died;* **therefore** *the car wouldn't start.*

connotation

associative meaning; the range of suggestion called up by a certain word. Apparent synonyms, such as *poor* and *underprivileged*, may have different connotations (cf. **denotation**).

context

the text surrounding a particular passage that helps to establish its meaning.

contraction

a word formed by combining and shortening two words: e.g., *isn't, can't, we're.*

coordinate construction

see **correlatives**.

copula verb

see **linking verb**.

correlatives (coordinates)

pairs of coordinating conjunctions: e.g., *either/or, neither/nor, not only/but.*

dangling modifier

a modifying word or phrase (often a participial phrase) that is not grammatically connected to any part of the sentence: e.g., **Walking to school**, *the street was slippery.*

demonstrative pronoun

a pronoun that points out something: e.g., (1) **This** *is his reason.* (2) **That** *looks like my lost earring.* When used to modify a noun or pronoun, a demonstrative pronoun becomes a kind of **pronominal adjective**: e.g., *this hat, those people.*

denotation

the literal or dictionary meaning of a word (cf. **connotation**).

diction

the choice of words with regard to their tone, degree of formality, or register. Formal diction is the language of orations and serious essays. The informal diction of everyday speech or conversational writing can, at its extreme, become slang.

discourse

talk, either oral or written. **Direct discourse** gives the actual words spoken or written: e.g., *Donne said,* **"No man is an island."** In writing, direct discourse is put in quotation marks.

Indirect discourse gives the meaning of the speech rather than the actual words. In writing, indirect discourse is not put in quotation marks: e.g., *He said that no one exists in an island of isolation.*

ellipsis marks
three spaced periods indicating an omission from a quoted passage.

endnote
a footnote or citation placed at the end of an essay or report.

essay
a literary composition on any subject. Some essays are descriptive or narrative, but in an academic setting most are expository (explanatory) or argumentative.

expletive
a grammatically meaningless exclamation or phrase. The most common expletives are the sentence beginnings *It is* and *There is (are)*.

exploratory writing
the informal writing done to help generate ideas before formal planning begins.

footnote
a citation placed at the bottom of a page or the end of the composition (cf. **endnote**).

fused sentence
see **run-on sentence**.

general language
language lacking specific details; abstract language.

gerund
a verbal (part-verb) that functions as a noun and is marked by an *-ing* ending: e.g., **Swimming** *can help you become fit.*

grammar
a study of the forms and relations of words, and of the rules governing their use in speech and writing.

hypothesis
a supposition or trial proposition made as a starting point for further investigation.

hypothetical instance
a supposed occurrence; often shown by a clause beginning with *if*.

indefinite article
see **article**.

independent clause
see **clause**.

indirect discourse
see **discourse**.

infinitive
a type of verbal not connected to any subject: e.g., *to ask*. The **base infinitive** omits the *to*: e.g., *ask*.

inflection
the change in the form of a word to indicate number, person, case, tense, or degree.

integrate
combine or blend together.

intensifier (qualifier)
a word that modifies and adds emphasis to another word or phrase: e.g.,**very** *tired*, **quite** *happy*, *I* **myself**.

interjection
a remark or exclamation interposed or thrown into a speech, usually accompanied by an exclamation mark: e.g., *Oh dear! Alas!*

interrogative sentence
a sentence that asks a question: e.g., *What is the time?*

intransitive verb
a verb that does not take a direct object: e.g., *fall, sleep, talk.*

italics
slanting type used for emphasis, replaced in typescript by underlining.

jargon
technical terms used unnecessarily or in inappropriate places: e.g., *peer-group interaction* for *friendship.*

linking verb (copula verb)
the verb *to be* used to join subject to complement: e.g., *The apples were ripe.*

literal meaning
the primary, or denotative, meaning of a word.

logical indicator
a word or phrase—usually a conjunction or conjunctive adverb— that shows the logical relation between sentences or clauses: e.g., *since, furthermore, therefore.*

misplaced modifier
a word or group of words that causes confusion or misreading because it is not placed next to the element it should modify: e.g., *I **only** ate the pie.* [Revised: *I ate **only** the pie.*]

modifier
a word or group of words that describes or limits another element in the sentence.

mood
(a) as a grammatical term, the form that shows a verb's function (indicative, imperative, interrogative, or subjunctive);
(b) when applied to literature generally, the state of mind or feeling shown.

non-restrictive modifier
see **restrictive modifier**.

noun
an inflected part of speech marking a person, place, thing, idea, action, or feeling, and usually serving as subject, object, or complement. A **common noun** is a general term: e.g., *dog, paper, automobile.* A **proper noun** is a specific name: e.g., *Mary, Sudbury, Skidoo.*

object
(a) a noun or pronoun that, when it completes the action of a verb, is called a **direct object**: e.g., *He passed the **puck**.* An **indirect object** is the person or thing receiving the direct object: e.g., *He passed the **puck*** (direct object) *to **Richard*** (indirect object).
(b) The noun or pronoun in a group of words beginning with a preposition; pronouns take the objective case: e.g., *at the* house, *about* **her**, *for* **me**.

objective complement
see **complement**.

objectivity
a disinterested stance; a position taken without personal bias or prejudice (cf. **subjectivity**).

outline
with regard to an essay or report, a brief sketch of the main parts; a written plan.

paragraph
a unit of sentences arranged logically to explain or describe an idea, event, or object; usually marked by indentation of the first line.

parallel wording
wording in which a series of items has a similar grammatical form: e.g., *At her marriage my grandmother promised* **to love, to honour, and to obey** *her husband.*

paraphrase
restate in different words.

parentheses
curved lines, enclosing and setting off a passage; not to be confused with square brackets.

parenthetical element
an interrupting word or phrase: e.g., *My musical career,* **if it can be called that**, *consisted of playing the triangle in kindergarten.*

participle
a verbal (part-verb) that functions as an adjective. Participles can be either **present**, usually marked by an *-ing* ending (e.g., *taking*), or **past** (*having taken*); they can also be passive (*having been taken*).

parts of speech
the major classes of words. Some grammarians include only function words (nouns, verbs, adjectives, and adverbs); others also include pronouns, prepositions, conjunctions, and interjections.

passive voice
see **voice**.

past participle
see **participle**.

periodic sentence
a sentence in which the normal order is inverted or an essential element suspended until the very end: e.g., *Out of the house, past the grocery store, through the school yard and down the railroad tracks* **raced the frightened boy**.

person
in grammar, the three classes of personal pronouns referring to the person speaking (first person), person spoken to (second person), and person spoken about (third person). With verbs, only the third person singular has a distinctive form.

personal pronoun
see **pronoun**.

phrase
a unit of words lacking a subject-predicate combination. The most common kind is the **prepositional phrase**—a unit comprising preposition plus object. Some modern grammarians also refer to the **single-word phrase**.

plural
indicating two or more in number. Nouns, pronouns, and verbs all have plural forms.

possessive case
see **case**.

prefix
a syllable placed in front of the root form of a word to make a new word: e.g., *pro-, in-, sub-* (cf. **suffix**).

preposition
a short word heading a unit of words containing an object, thus forming a **prepositional phrase**: e.g., **under** *the tree*, **before** *my time*.

pronoun
a word that stands in for a noun.

punctuation
a conventional system of signs used to indicate stops or divisions in a sentence and to make meaning clearer: e.g., comma, period, semicolon, etc.

reference works
material consulted when preparing an essay or report.

referent (antecedent)
the noun for which a pronoun stands.

relative clause
a clause headed by a relative pronoun: e.g., *the man* **who came to dinner** *is my uncle.*

relative pronoun
who, which, what, that, or their compounds beginning an adjective or noun clause: e.g., *the house* **that** *Jack built*; **whatever** *you say.*

restrictive element
a phrase or clause that identifies or is essential to the meaning of a term: e.g., *The book* **that I need** *is lost.* It should not be set off by commas. A non-restrictive element is not needed to identify the term and is usually set off by commas: e.g., *This book,* **which I got from my aunt***, is one of my favourites.*

register
the degree of formality in word choice and sentence structure.

run-on sentence
a sentence that goes on beyond the point where it should have stopped. The term covers both the **comma splice** (two sentences joined by a comma) and the **fused sentence** (two sentences joined without any punctuation between them).

sentence
a grammatical unit that includes both a subject and a predicate. The end of a sentence is marked by a period.

sentence fragment
a group of words lacking either a subject or a verb; an incomplete sentence.

simple sentence
a sentence made up of only one clause: e.g., *Joan climbed the tree.*

slang
colloquial speech, not considered part of standard English; often used in a special sense by a particular group: e.g., *gross* for *disgusting*; *gig* as a musician's term.

split infinitive
a construction in which a word is placed between *to* and the base verb: e.g., *to completely finish.*

squinting modifier
a kind of misplaced modifier; one that could be connected to elements on either side, making meaning ambiguous: e.g., *When he wrote the letter* **finally** *his boss thanked him.*

standard English
the English currently spoken or written by literate people over a wide geographical area.

subject
in grammar, the noun or noun equivalent about which something is predicated; that part of a clause with which the verb agrees: e.g., **They** *swim every day when the* **pool** *is open.*

subjectivity
a personal stance, not impartial (cf. **objectivity**).

subjunctive
see **mood**.

subordinate clause
see **clause**.

subordinating conjunction
see **conjunction**.

subordination
making one clause in a sentence dependent on another.

suffix
an addition placed at the end of a word to form a derivative: e.g., *prepare—prepara***tion**; *sing—sing***ing** (cf. **prefix**).

synonym
a word with the same dictionary meaning as another word: e.g., *begin* and *commence.*

syntax
sentence construction; the grammatical relations of words.

tense
the time reference of verbs.

thesis statement
a one-sentence assertion that gives the central argument of an essay or thesis.

topic sentence
the sentence in a paragraph that expresses the main or controlling idea.

theme
a recurring or dominant idea.

transition word
a word that shows the logical relation between sentences or parts of a sentence and thus helps to signal the change from one idea to another: e.g., *therefore, also, accordingly.*

transitive verb
one that takes an object: e.g., *hit, bring, cover.*

usage
accepted practice.

verb
that part of a predicate expressing an action, state of being, or condition, telling what a subject is or does. Verbs inflect to show tense (time). The principal parts of a verb are the three basic forms from which all tenses are made: the base infinitive, the past tense, and the past participle.

verbal
a word that is similar in form to a verb but does not function as one: a participle, a gerund, or an infinitive.

voice
the form of a verb that shows whether the subject acted (active voice) or was acted upon (passive voice): e.g., *He* **hit** *the ball* (active). *The ball* **was hit** *by him* (passive). Only transitive verbs (verbs taking objects) can be passive.

Appendix:
some additional
exercises

Now that you know everything you need to know about making sense in social science, try answering the following questions. In each instance, (a) select an appropriate design; (b) identify the key variables and draw a flow chart to depict your theory; (c) indicate how you would measure each variable; and (d) deal with the main alternative arguments.

1. What are the likely effects of a national insurance scheme to provide legal services to everyone who needs them?
2. What social attitudes and behaviours tend to fuel inflation?
3. What factors affect the formation of political alliances between nation-states?
4. What is the process by which a workplace becomes unionized? What factors are *necessary* to unionization (i.e., always present), what factors merely *sufficient* (i.e., occasionally present, and able to bring about the result)?
5. How, historically, did the ownership and the control of business organizations become separated? What are the consequences of this separation?
6. Why are native people from some bands more likely than native people from other bands to work off the reserve?
7. What factors determine the rate of intermarriage between two ethnic groups?
8. What social, economic, or political problems are caused by fluctuations in population size?
9. How has U.S. domination of the Canadian economy affected regionalism?
10. What social problems are likely in future to be solved through the use of complex technology?

Index

NOTE: Grammatical terms not listed here are explained in the glossary.

Notes

Notes

Notes

Notes

Notes

Notes